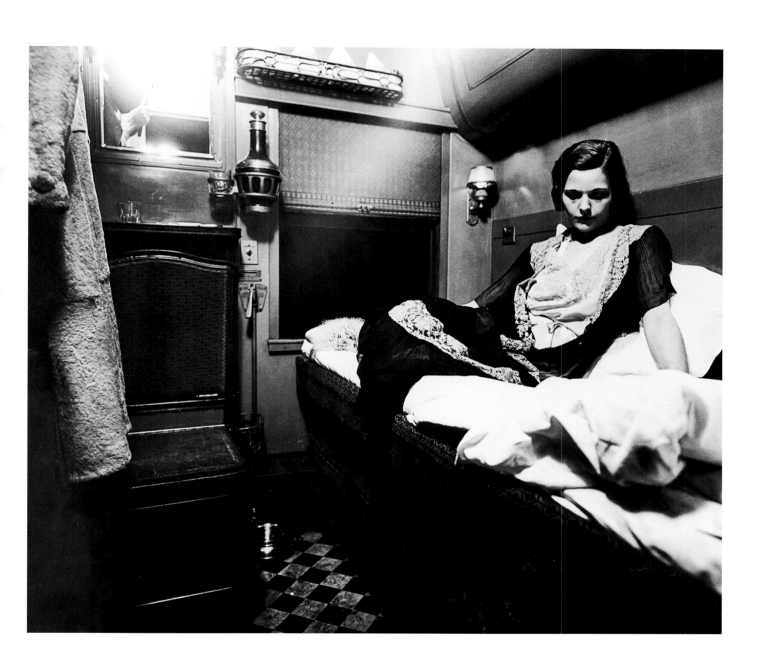

THE CARS OF
PULLMAN

JOE WELSH, BILL HOWES & KEVIN J. HOLLAND

Voyageur Press

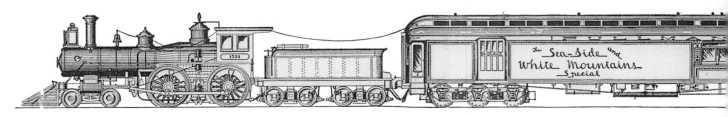

In Memory of Alan Bradley

First published in 2010 by Voyageur Press, an imprint of MBI Publishing Company, 400 First Avenue North, Suite 300, Minneapolis, MN 55401 USA

Copyright © 2010 by Joe Welsh, Bill Howes & Kevin J. Holland

The information in this book is true and complete to the best of our knowledge. All recommendations are made without any guarantee on the part of the author or Publisher, who also disclaims any liability incurred in connection with the use of this data or specific details.

We recognize, further, that some words, model names, and designations mentioned herein are the property of the trademark holder. We use them for identification purposes only.
This is not an official publication.

Voyageur Press titles are also available at discounts in bulk quantity for industrial or sales-promotional use. For details write to Special Sales Manager at MBI Publishing Company, 400 First Avenue North, Suite 300, Minneapolis, MN 55401 USA.

To find out more about our books, visit us online at www.voyageurpress.com.

Library of Congress Cataloging-in-Publication Data

Welsh, Joe.
    The cars of Pullman / Joe Welsh, Bill Howes, and Kevin J. Holland.
    p. cm.
    Includes bibliographical references and index.
    ISBN 978-0-7603-3587-1 (hb w/ jkt)
    1. Pullman cars–History. 2. Railroad passenger cars–
    History. I. Howes, Bill. II. Holland, Kevin J. III. Title.
    TF459.W43 2010
    625.2'3–dc22
                        2009024488

Front cover: For decades, the New York Central's *20th Century Limited*, seen here in 1948, was America's most prestigious train. Pullman observation cars *Sandy Creek* (pictured) and its sister, *Hickory Creek*, will offer these passengers at New York City's Grand Central Terminal fine views all the way to Chicago. *NYC photo*

Frontispiece: The Pullman single-bedroom accommodation debuted in 1927. Compact yet private, they gave single travelers the privacy they sought. *Pullman photo, courtesy Bob's Photo*

Title pages: Mother and son enjoy the comforts of bunk beds on the Lackawanna Railroad's Pullman sleeping car *Tioughnioga* in 1949. *ACF Industries*

Back cover: Its neon tail sign glowing a welcome through the steam, the Pullman observation car of the westbound *California Zephyr* pauses at Omaha, Nebraska, in November 1969. *Bob Schmidt*

Acquisitions Editor: Dennis Pernu
Design Manager: Katie Sonmor
Design and layout: Cindy Samargia Laun and Sarah Bennett
Cover design: Matthew Simmons

Printed in China

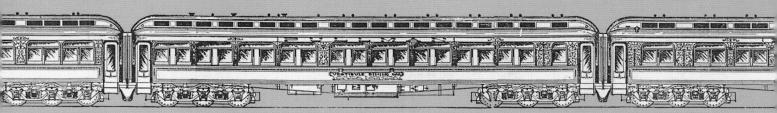

CONTENTS

INTRODUCTION

THE PULLMAN COMPANY, FOUNDED BY GEORGE MORTIMER PULLMAN, served the U.S. travel market from 1867 to 1968. Though a major player in American passenger railroading for more than a century, Pullman was not a railroad. The company built, owned, and leased a large fleet of sleeping and parlor cars, which it provided to the railroads under contract. The railroads handled the reservations and carried travelers from place to place aboard Pullman cars. Pullman was essentially a giant hotel company. As a result of mergers, reorganizations, and court cases, the company name went through several iterations. For the most part, in this book it is referred to simply as "Pullman."

The composition of Pullman's car fleet was as diverse as the destinations of its cars. Originally providing services aboard a fleet of ornate wooden cars, Pullman and the accommodations it offered expanded in response to demand. For example, Pullman's fleet transitioned from wood construction to steel beginning in earnest in 1910.

The orderly world in which Pullman was a primary provider of transportation in the United States began to collapse in late 1929. Suddenly, the great company, which had once enjoyed a virtual monopoly in its market, began losing money as people stopped traveling or shifted to less costly options, such as travel by railway coach or private auto. In fact, more than 40 percent of Pullman's patronage evaporated between 1929 and 1932. To lure them back, the company air-conditioned and rebuilt hundreds of its cars, and began the slow process of streamlining its fleet.

Other changes were in the wind. As a result of a 1944 federal antitrust decision against the company (a suit initiated by manufacturing competitor The Budd Company in 1940), Pullman Incorporated was ordered to divest itself of either its manufacturing arm (Pullman-Standard Car Manufacturing Company) or its operating arm (Pullman Company). The choice

was easy: Pullman kept the lucrative manufacturing business, which was busy churning out passenger and freight cars for railroad fleets worn down by war traffic. The Pullman Company was purchased by a group of 57 (later 59) railroads. This new Pullman Company kept a fleet of more than 2,800 heavyweight sleeping, lounge, and parlor cars, and 6 lightweight cars for pool service. The rest of the fleet was sold to the railroads that owned The Pullman Company and was leased back to Pullman, which operated and maintained the fleet under contract.

However, the rise in popularity of the auto and commercial airliner cut heavily into Pullman's remaining business. Pullman ridership declined steadily after 1946, with the exception of the Korean War years of 1951 and 1952. Overall, Pullman ridership dropped by more than four million from 1950 to 1955. In response, Pullman and the railroads modernized significantly. More than 4,400 lightweight railroad passenger cars were constructed, and the industry spent more than $1.3 billion (in 1950s' dollars) on new equipment. The new cars were made of lightweight metals, streamlined in appearance, and finished in attractive colors or stainless steel. Among the cars built postwar, the railroads purchased 1,603 modern lightweight sleeping cars for lease to Pullman.

By the late 1960s, the speed of the airplane and convenience of the highway had defeated the intercity railroad passenger train. The numbers tell the story. In 1946, Pullman operated more than 5,500 cars. By December 31, 1968, when Pullman closed its doors to passengers in the United States and Canada, it ran just 425 cars. By mid-1969, after 102 years of service, Pullman was out of the business of providing car maintenance in the United States and Canada. Pullman passenger service in Mexico ended in late 1970. The great company that had once been a household name was relegated to the history books.

The West's First All Room Train

I N addition to its many other unique distinctions, the new streamlined *Lark* is the West's first train with private room accommodations only. Its roomettes, double bedrooms, compartments and drawing rooms are the newest and finest in America, and embody the latest refinements in travel comfort and luxury.

It costs surprisingly little to travel on the *Lark*. There is no extra rail fare and the Pullman charge is much less than you'd imagine. For example, two people can occupy a *Lark* bedroom between San Francisco-Oakland and Los Angeles for a Pullman charge of $3.15 each—exactly the same as you would pay for a lower berth!

Compartments have a convertible sofa-bed and upper berth (both 6 feet 5 inches long and of standard berth width), a comfortable lounge chair, complete toilet facilities, clothes locker and ample space for luggage.

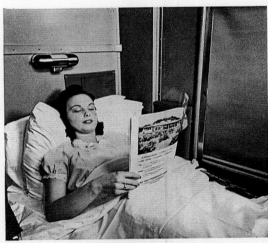

Roomettes are completely equipped private rooms for one person, have a comfortable wall bed with mattress of soft foam rubber, complete toilet facilities, full-length mirror and individual ventilation, heat and light controls.

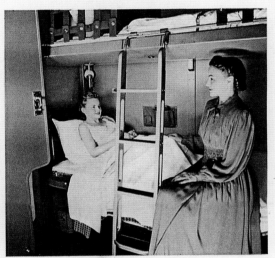

Double Bedrooms on the new *Lark* are ideal for two persons, are also popular with people traveling alone. They have a bed, upper berth, complete toilet facilities, writing desk, generous closet, three mirrors.

There's a planned place for everything in a roomette: clothes locker, luggage rack, mirrored cabinet.

Roomette bed swings down from wall all ready to sleep in (you can lower bed yourself if you wish).

The Friendly Southern Pacific

Drawing Rooms easily accommodate three people (five if necessary), have a big seat and two movable, folding-type lounge chairs. Sleeping facilities: a bed, upper berth, wall bed. Private toilet in adjoining room.

1859

"OLD No. 9" THE FIRST PULLMAN CAR The first Pullman sleeper, built 1859, was a reconstructed day coach, 40 feet long or about half the present length. Except wheels and axles, it was practically all wood. The roof was flat and so low a tall man was liable to bump his head. The seats were immovable; two small wood-burning stoves furnished heat. Lighted with candles, it had at each end a small toilet room large enough for one person, with tin wash basin in the open and water from the drinking faucet. There were ten upper and ten lower berths; mattresses and blankets, but no sheets. But it was the best yet.

1865

THE FIRST REAL PULLMAN SLEEPING CAR First modern sleeper, built 1865, THE PIONEER; much longer, higher, wider, than predecessors; railroad bridges and platforms were changed to permit its passage. Here first came the raised upper deck and folding upper berth. Heated from hot air furnace under floor; lighted with candles, ventilated through deck windows. Two compartments at each end; eight sections; roomy washroom; black walnut woodwork, much inlay and many mirrors. Fully carpeted; French plush upholstery; good beds, ample bedding. Note the 16 wheels: an experiment tried at this period but later abandoned in favor of 12.

1876

THE STEADY MARCH OF PROGRESS CENTENNIAL YEAR—1876—opened a period of further progress. The car's length grew from 58 to 70 feet. Oil lamps superseded candles. Air brakes appeared, making for greater speed and safety. A hot water heating system replaced stoves and furnaces. Six-wheel trucks were definitely adopted and overhead tanks with gravity supply system afforded water. Interior finish was in walnut, with carving, inlaying and lacquer work characteristic of the period.

1887

THE CAR VESTIBULE APPEARS The car vestibule, marking an historical advance, appeared in 1887, strictly a Pullman invention. At first it merely enclosed a narrow passage between cars, to be widened later to full car width. It greatly enhanced comfort and safety. With twelve sections, drawing room, and smoking room, high backed seats, mahogany finish, much carving and ornamentation, higher windows, rich carpets and upholstery, and increasing elegance throughout, the Pullman was now blossoming into the full glory of the later Victorian period.

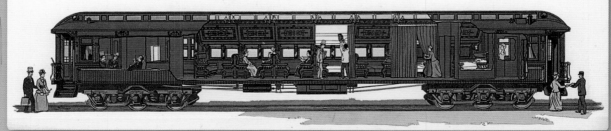

A 1930s brochure illustrates the evolution of the Pullman car. *Pullman*

1907

THE ALL-STEEL CAR APPEARS No other advance in car building made so much for safety, up to this date, as all-steel construction. Following the first experimental steel car, in 1907, the type was adopted in general service in 1910. Length 74 feet; full vestibule; 12 sections, drawing room and smoking room; steel sheathed outside; electric light from axle device; low pressure vapor heat system. Interiors were by this time becoming more quiet, moderate and tasteful, with plain mottled finish, green frieze plush upholstery and green carpets. This was the period of standardization.

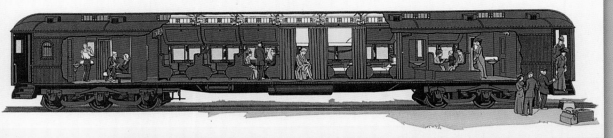

1917

WATER, HEAT AND LIGHT CIRCUITS By 1917 the Pullman car contained innumerable hidden mechanisms, concealed devices, ingenuities of construction, electrical wizardries and accessories, created and installed by experts to give the maximum of comfort and luxury to the twentieth century traveler. A single Pullman car contained nearly a mile of insulated copper wire; over half a mile of pipes, and conduits; a maze of batteries, switches, valves, switch boards, dynamos, motors, ventilators, push buttons, call bells, regulators, signaling apparatus, controls, and other appurtenances.

▬▬ COLD WATER ▬▬ HOT WATER ▬▬ STEAM ▬▬ ELECTRICAL UNITS

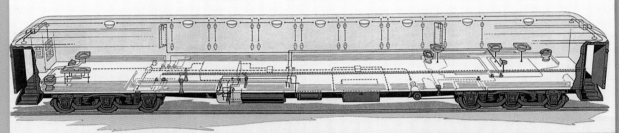

1927

THE SINGLE ROOM CAR The single room car, for over-night journeys, is a particular luxury to a large class of travelers. It contains 14 rooms, each for a single passenger, with full toilet facilities, stationary bed across the car, folding washstand with mirror and side lights above; drop shelf for writing or serving meals. Luggage space under bed, and in roomy racks. Cheval mirror inside door. Air intake in door, electric fan, thermos water bottle, individual heat control. The bed has box springs and spring mattress. Two or more rooms can be used *en suite* if desired.

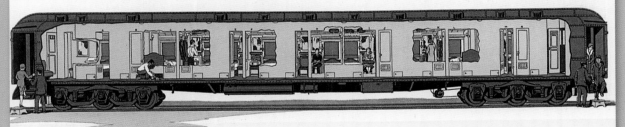

1929

AIR-CONDITIONING SYSTEM With the introduction of the first successfully operated air-conditioned sleeping car in 1929, the Pullman Company rapidly added this innovation in travel comfort to its equipment and by 1937 operated over 50% of all the air-conditioned passenger cars in the United States. The mechanical devices employed in air-conditioning indicated in the car are as follows:

1. INTAKES
2. FILTERS
3. BLOWERS
4. COOLING COIL OR EVAPORATOR
5. HEATING RADIATOR
6. HOLDOVER COIL
7. DUCTS
8. GRILLED OUTLETS
9. COMPRESSOR
10. CONDENSER
11. RECEIVING TANK
12. DOUBLE PULLEY
13. DRIVE BELTS
14. BEVEL GEAR UNIT
15. DRIVE SHAFT
16. SPEED CONTROL
17. STANDBY MOTOR
18. TANK FOR AUXILIARY HOLDOVER SYSTEM
19. COOLING COILS
20. LOWER BERTH NOZZLE OUTLET

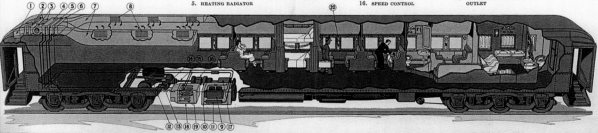

THE PULLMAN COMPANY:

AN OVERVIEW

ONE OF THE MOST FAMOUS BUSINESSES IN AMERICAN HISTORY, Pullman was incorporated in Illinois in February 1867 as Pullman's Palace Car Company. The organization was renamed The Pullman Company in 1900.

While Pullman was a major player in American passenger railroading for more than a century, it was not a railroad. Pullman owned no tracks, aside from those at its own shops. It didn't possess powerful mainline steam locomotives or road diesels, and it didn't run its own trains. Instead the company built, owned, or leased a large fleet of sleeping and parlor cars that it provided to the railroads under contract. The railroads handled the reservations and carried passengers from place to place aboard Pullman cars.

Heavyweight Pullman *Barnard College* carries the markers of the Rio Grande's *Royal Gorge* at Pueblo, Colorado, in 1956.
Krambles–Peterson Archive

By March 1907, when Pullman built its first steel car, the company had become an American institution. Railroads focused their attention on moving trains and generally relied on other companies to feed and care for their first-class customers. Pullman cars were assigned to Pullman lines that linked two endpoints, usually functioning within the same train as the cars of the operating railroad. Between 1867 and 1907, American railroad track mileage expanded from 39,000 miles to 229,000 miles. Routes became longer as the traveling public's horizons expanded to overnight and far-reaching destinations. The sleeping car and dining car, once curiosities, were now essential elements of rail travel.

As one of many sleeping and first-class car companies that sprung up in the mid- to late 1800s, Pullman didn't invent the product it offered; it perfected it. At the same time, Pullman's aggressive business practices earned its supremacy. The construction and operation of a fleet of state-of-the-art, often ornate wooden sleeping and dining cars, as well as private cars for use on the railroad, were the principal services Pullman provided. At the end of 1899, when it purchased its last major competitor, the Wagner Palace Car Company, for a then whopping $36 million, Pullman stood alone as a virtual monopoly. At that point, Pullman controlled almost 90 percent of railroad sleeping car service in North America.

The first decade of the twentieth century was the most profitable in Pullman history as the company's traffic tripled and its assets doubled. By 1910, the company's fleet comprised nearly 3,700 sleepers, more than 600 lower-quality tourist sleepers, over 600 parlor cars, 25 dining cars, and 34 private cars. By the end of the 1920s, Pullman operated 9,800 cars staffed by 10,500 porters, attendants, and maids. During the high point of overnight rail travel in the 1920s, Pullman carried millions of passengers per year.

By manufacturing, maintaining, and staffing its cars, Pullman offered a practical way for railroads to provide first-class service despite variable traffic trends. For example, Pullman could easily shift its fleet of cars and onboard personnel around the country in response to fluctuating demand. In the winter, hundreds of Pullman cars were assigned to service on rival railroads, such as the Seaboard Air Line (SAL)

and Atlantic Coast Line (ACL), which ferried passengers from the frigid North down to sunny Florida. When the Florida traffic declined each spring, the same cars were reassigned to other railroads to serve the growing summer travel demand to the American West. This national fleet of cars precluded the need for individual railroads to maintain larger staffs and car fleets, which might have been idle or underemployed for much of the year.

As a result of this national-fleet strategy, Pullman's cars went everywhere. In its heyday, Pullman's enormous fleet of cars could be found in almost every

Pullman car *Kankakee* with 12 sections and 1 drawing room brings up the rear of Pennsylvania Railroad's *Admiral* in May 1952. Built in October 1922, *Kankakee* was never painted in anything other than Pullman green. The car was sold to Illinois Central in December 1948. Her best days behind her, she was withdrawn from Pullman lease in March 1954. *R. V. Mehlenbeck, Krambles–Peterson Archive*

nook and cranny of the United States, as well as select destinations in Mexico and Canada. At the height of Pullman's operations in the late 1920s, an average Pullman car traveled 136,500 miles per year. The movements of a car were largely dependent on its type and assignment. Some specialty cars, such as observation cars, rarely, if ever, ventured from the train to which they were specifically assigned. Other cars, which had floor plans more attuned to serve the shifting demands of Pullman service, could be found almost anywhere. For example, in March 1929, the compartment and drawing room sleeper *Glen Alta*, assigned to Pullman's roving pool of cars, visited Toronto, Miami, Los Angeles, and New York. The *Glen Alta* encountered temperatures ranging from 6 degrees to 86 degrees—all in one month. The car began 1929 in New York City and ended the year in remote Key West, Florida.

While the *Glen Alta* was seeing much of North America, other cars—such as *John Adams*, firmly assigned to parlor service on the busy 226-mile New York–Washington line—might make just one short roundtrip a day. Likewise, *Assembly Hall* and its sisters—Pullman observation cars assigned to the prestigious *Broadway Limited* of the Pennsylvania Railroad (PRR)—rarely, if ever, left that train's consist or route between New York and Chicago.

This orderly world in which Pullman was a primary provider of transportation in the United States began to collapse with the onset

The famous-name trains got the publicity, but Pullman earned its reputation by providing service on a host of unsung overnight trains. In these views taken in late evening hours in April 1968, Gulf, Mobile & Ohio's *Midnight Special* prepares to depart Chicago Union Station on its overnight run to St. Louis. In the foreground (bottom) is sleeping car *Culver White*, one of four postwar Pullman sleepers delivered to GM&O by American Car and Foundry. *Both Bob Schmidt*

of the Great Depression in late 1929. The effect on Pullman was dramatic. Forty percent of its patronage vanished between 1929 and 1932. Travelers switched to cheaper modes of transportation, such as railway coach or private auto. Realizing it was losing money, Pullman air-conditioned and rebuilt hundreds of its cars and began the process, albeit slowly, of streamlining its own fleet to recapture its lost customers.

Ridership for Pullman and the railroads bounced back after 1941. As World War II progressed, Pullman and the railroads were swamped with demand, finding themselves playing the role of unsung heroes on the home front, just as they did during World War I. About 125 million passengers, including troops, traveled 98 billion miles in Pullman cars during World War II. Between November 1945 and June 1946, more than 5.5 million veterans arrived home in Pullman cars.

Other changes had an impact on ridership levels. As a result of a 1944 federal antitrust decision against Pullman (a suit triggered by manufacturing competitor The Budd Company in 1940), the company was ordered to divest itself of either its manufacturing arm or its operating arm. The choice was easy. Pullman kept the lucrative manufacturing business, which would be busy churning out passenger and freight cars for railroad fleets worn down by war traffic.

Pullman's operating company went up for sale and was eventually purchased by a group of 57 (later 59) railroads. The new version of the Pullman operating company kept a fleet of more than 2,800 heavyweight sleeping, lounge, and parlor cars, and 6 lightweight cars for pool service. The rest of its car fleet was sold to the railroads and then leased back to the new Pullman operating company. The railroads now owned the new first-class sleeping and parlor cars that were built after the war. Pullman leased and operated them. All in all, the process of running the new company differed very little from before the split. However, the new Pullman operating company found itself with increasing competition from autos and airplanes, and the labor-intensive railroad passenger industry began to crack.

In response, Pullman and many railroads accelerated the pace of modernization by introducing thousands of new streamlined passenger cars.

During the years following 1946, ridership decreased dramatically. Then, Pullman ridership dropped by more than four million from 1950 to 1955. More important, Pullman's average annual operating

Milwaukee Road's famous *Pioneer Limited* pauses at Milwaukee, Wisconsin, on its nocturnal journey from the Twin Cities to Chicago. *Russ Porter*

expenses exceeded its revenues every year from 1946 to 1968, with 1948 the lone exception. When revenue from a Pullman line exceeded expenses, the railroad generally kept 75 percent of the profit and Pullman got the remainder. Yet when expenses exceeded revenues, the railroad was required to make up the deficit to Pullman. This latter point, coupled with the

fact that the railroads owned Pullman, explains why Pullman service shrank so fast when profits dried up in the 1950s and 1960s. The railroads often were not inclined to maintain the service.

This problem was particularly acute on Pullman car routes that served short distances in marginal ridership markets. In 1957, for example, the Delaware,

Lackawanna & Western Railroad (DL&W), which offered Pullman service to a number of smaller communities in upstate New York, such as Elmira and Binghamton, lost nearly $186,000 on Pullman. Not a single DL&W–Pullman line of the seven in operation that year made a profit.

Clearly, one of the largest factors of ridership decline was the proliferation of the automobile and auto travel. Americans, tired of being cooped up by wartime gas and tire rationing and beginning to enjoy new levels of disposable income, bought 37 million cars between 1946 and 1954. In 1956, Congress and President Dwight D. Eisenhower created the Interstate Highway System, which ultimately revolutionized travel within the United States. Travelers now had smooth highways to use, making travel easier and faster, and could often find a new Howard Johnson's Motor Lodge or Holiday Inn not far off the road at the end of their day.

For those not enticed to travel by highway, the friendly skies were opening up as a more viable travel option. By the time the jet airliner began entering service in 1958 and 1959, challenging even the best and most profitable trains to the biggest cities, the die was cast. For example, the average flight from Philadelphia to Chicago took a little more than two hours. Flying above the weather, the new jets were more reliable and more comfortable than piston aircraft. Despite wonderful first-class service, the same trip by rail in a Pullman car took 14 ½ hours. For Pullman's primary customer, the businessman, there was little doubt which way he would travel. Time was money.

As embattled railroads continued to terminate trains and Pullman services, the massive support organization necessary to operate the Pullman fleet was serving fewer and fewer remaining car lines. In 1956, Pullman parlor car service ended. PRR, New Haven Railroad (NH), and Wabash Railroad were the last

With a pedigree dating to 1911, Illinois Central's legendary *Panama Limited* was one of the last all-Pullman trains in America. The southbound *Panama*, train No. 5, is pictured speeding to New Orleans at Homewood, Illinois, in April 1960. *Dave Ingles*

Sleeper-observation car *Gulfport* punctuates the Illinois Central's southbound *Panama Limited* at Homewood, Illinois, south of Chicago in April 1960. *Dave Ingles*

three railroads to use Pullman parlor service. Any remaining parlor services were provided by the railroads themselves. As its sleeping car demand shrank and costs rose, New York Central (NYC), one of the country's largest railroads, dropped Pullman sleeper service in 1958, choosing to operate its own sleeping cars to save money. Pullman was trapped in a downward economic spiral.

By the late 1960s, the speed of air travel and the convenience of the highway had all but defeated the intercity railroad passenger train. In 1946, Pullman operated more than 5,500 cars. By December 31, 1968, when Pullman closed its doors to passengers in the United States and Canada, it ran just 425 cars. By mid-1969, Pullman got out of the business of providing car maintenance in the United States and Canada, after 102 years of service. Pullman passenger service in Mexico ended in late 1970.

FLEET COMPOSITION

The composition of Pullman's car fleet was as diverse as the destinations of its cars. Originally providing its services in a group of ornate wooden cars, the Pullman roster and the accommodations it offered evolved in response to demand. Beginning in earnest in 1910, the Pullman fleet transitioned to steel construction due to a growing concern about the durability of wooden cars and their ability to withstand both collision and fire. There were 2,100 steel Pullman cars in service by 1913, representing a third of Pullman's total passenger car fleet.

By World War II, Pullman's car fleet contained a wide selection of room types and car types. These types ran the gamut from older heavyweight sleepers with traditional interiors, and simple heavyweight tourist sleepers with rudimentary accommodations, to brand-new and innovative lightweight cars running

Pullman observation cars for the *North Coast Limited* (left) destined for the Pacific Northwest and the *California Zephyr* (right) headed for Oakland/San Francisco take a breather at Burlington's Chicago coach yard. *Alan Bradley*

on the top trains in the country. Recently rebuilt heavyweight cars with floor plans and accommodations better suited to a market that had been evolving for some time also were part of the mix. Pullman's revenue fleet in the twentieth century can be most easily broken into four major types of cars: sleeping cars, parlor cars, dining and restaurant cars, and private cars for lease.

SLEEPING CARS

The vast majority of Pullman's cars were sleeping cars. In 1930, when Pullman's fleet was at or near its peak, the company rostered 7,982 sleepers and an

additional 281 tourist sleepers. That same year, Pullman carried more than 20.7 million revenue passengers in its sleepers, while another 365,000 rode in its tourist cars. Roughly half of Pullman's nearly 8,000 sleeping cars at the time contained a standardized floor plan with 12 sections and 1 drawing room (12-1). This "section" was Pullman's earliest regular accommodation. It contained two sofa-type seats facing each other so that two people, often strangers, could hardly avoid eye contact. In the evening, the same space was converted into a lower berth and an upper berth separated from the aisle only by heavy, temporary curtains. The upper-berth passenger, who

Chesapeake & Ohio 10-roomette, 6-double-bedroom sleeping car *City of Newport* pauses at Ashland, Kentucky, in the consist of train No. 1, *The George Washington,* in November 1970. Its days as a Pullman-operated car were over but the sleeper still carried Pullman on its letterboard. *Bob Schmidt*

paid less than the lower, rode facing backward during the day and endured the nearly impossible task of dressing and undressing in a space not much larger than a coffin at night. Not surprisingly, the upper berth fell from favor. For example in the 1930s, PRR—Pullman's largest customer—revealed that while it could fill 77 percent of the more spacious lower berths in its sections, it could only fill 18 percent of its upper berths.

This shift in customer preference, coupled with the sharp decline in first-class ridership resulting from the economic impacts of the Depression, forced Pullman to improvise and change. The company

devised a handful of short-term solutions, including the single-occupancy section, which offered a whole section to one passenger for a slightly elevated fare. Pullman also introduced the duplex single room, an "upstairs-downstairs" arrangement of rooms that partially overlapped each other to save floor space. The duplex roomette, a variation of the duplex single room, was quite popular in the years following World War II. Pullman's most successful prewar innovation, the roomette, was a fully enclosed space for one, complete with a picture window, sink, and toilet in a room surrounded by solid walls and accessible via a real door. Pullman's larger rooms for two persons (compartments) and three persons (drawing rooms), which had proliferated prior to the Depression, remained in large numbers in subsequent years and were retained in the new lightweight car designs of the early 1930s.

As the economy spiraled downward, though, railroads had a more difficult time filling these expensive accommodations. The double bedroom debuted in 1930 and proved successful until the end of Pullman service in the 1960s. Originally an outgrowth of the single-bedroom cars introduced in 1927, the double bedroom proved to be a near-ideal accommodation in price and space for two passengers. As Pullman rebuilt older cars, it often added double bedrooms to them. When the company built new streamlined equipment, the double bedroom was incorporated into configurations such as all-bedroom cars, roomette cars, and bedroom lounge cars. Often these accommodations were arranged together en suite, with

a folding wall that allowed for the creation of one large room that slept four passengers.

Pullman's largest and perhaps rarest accommodation, the master room, slept two and could only be found on a handful of the top trains in the country. The spacious room, which came complete with a full shower, was incorporated into observation cars for the PRR's *Broadway Limited* and the New York Central's *20th Century Limited*, as well as within the midtrain lounge of *The Crescent*, a joint operation of the Pennsylvania Railroad, Southern Railway, Atlanta & West Point, and Louisville & Nashville.

The sleeper/lounge combined overnight accommodations with a lounge where drinks and even modest meals were dispensed. These cars were common in both the steel heavyweight car era (1910–1932) and the lightweight period (1932–1968). The cars offered lounge space for first-class passengers while including revenue-generating sleeping space to boost profits.

The famous Great Northern streamliner the *Empire Builder* is shown circa 1956. The going-away view shows the train's Pullman sleeper-observation car, two Pullman sleeping cars, a *Great Dome* lounge car, a diner, and more sleeping cars. *Russ Porter*

The Northern Pacific's *North Coast Limited* is shown paused at Livingston, Montana, in June 1962. Pullman sleeper-observation car No. 390 brings up the rear as a Pullman porter in a white jacket assists passengers. *George Krambles, Krambles–Peterson Archive*

Milwaukee Road's *Gallatin River* is shown serving as the Milwaukee set-out sleeper for the railroad's famous *Pioneer Limited*. The car was one of eight sleeping cars delivered to the Milwaukee in 1948 with 8 duplex roomettes, 6 roomettes, and 4 double bedrooms. Their floor plan was unusual in that the least expensive accommodations, the duplex roomettes, were located in the center of the car, where the ride was best. The car is loading No. 47, the eastbound set-out car. *Russ Porter*

Pullman & the Sleeping Car

GEORGE MORTIMER PULLMAN DIDN'T INVENT THE SLEEPING CAR. Basic (and initially rather crude) sleeping accommodations had been available sporadically on trains for some 20 years at the time of Pullman's first venture into the field, in 1858. Legend has it that Pullman was inspired to improve railroad sleeping accommodations by a nocturnal trip he endured in 1853 traveling between Westfield and Buffalo, New York, a trip on which he got little rest on the car's uncomfortable bunk bed.

Pullman and an associate, Benjamin C. Field, drawing heavily upon the ideas and experience of others plus their own imagination and technical skills, contracted to remodel two railroad coaches with "sections" of retractable upper and lower berths to permit the cars to be run as coaches by day and transformed into sleeping accommodations at night. The two modified a pair of coaches from the Chicago, Alton & St. Louis (CA&StL) for overnight travel. Field had recently acquired patents from T. T. Woodruff, an established car builder and sleeping car concessionaire. CA&StL cars No. 9 and No. 19 were selected and outfitted with positionable berths— probably operated with ropes and counterweights— above two rows of paired coach seats (or sections) that faced each other. The seat backs were hinged so they could be folded down to form a lower bunk, on which a mattress could be placed. Thus, a day coach could be converted quickly for reasonably comfortable nighttime travel. Car No. 9, with what is believed to have been 10 two-berth sections, made its inaugural run from Bloomington, Illinois, to Chicago on the night of September 1, 1859, followed later in the year by a similar car, No. 19. Train crewmen provided passengers with blankets. It was a modest but welcome improvement in sleep accommodations.

Although Field completed a third conversion for the CA&StL, the Civil War effectively interrupted further development in sleeping car design. In the meantime, George Pullman had moved to Colorado to engage in the sale and transportation of supplies in support of the silver mining boom. He returned to Chicago in 1863 with more ideas and the financial means to build upon them. He envisioned a time after the war when the railroad network would rapidly expand to open the Midwest and West to agriculture, mining, and commerce, and to rebuild the war-torn South. Pullman gathered that more Americans would be traveling and their trips would be longer.

Pullman and Field also recognized that further improvement in sleeping car technology was needed, but only with a car designed from the wheels up. This led to the construction of Car A, later named *Pioneer*, which was completed in 1865. Although details are sketchy, the car may have been somewhat taller and wider than a normal car, perhaps to more readily accommodate and ventilate the 12 two-tiered sections with their foldaway upper berths, or to showcase the car's lavish decor. In Pullman Company mythology, it took a last-minute assignment as the final leg (Chicago to Springfield) of Abraham Lincoln's funeral train from Washington, D.C., to gain acceptance for the car's outside dimensions.

As unconventional as the *Pioneer* was, there is little doubt that it established a standard that, with continual refinement, defined railroad sleeping car service for the next 100 years. To initially attract clients for the sleeping car, Pullman and other entrepreneurs aggressively promoted a level of elegance and comfort aboard trains that was equal to that of a first-class hotel. Pullman was soon entering into operating contracts with railroads to offer the public, for a supplemental charge, luxurious parlor seating by day, sleeping accommodations at night, and fine onboard dining.

George M. Pullman's first sleeping car, No. 9 of the Chicago, Alton & St. Louis, was rebuilt into this configuration in the railroad's shops in Bloomington, Illinois. The car made its first revenue run on September 1, 1859. This view shows a replica of the car. *H. C. Fall collection, Railway & Locomotive Historical Society*

PARLOR CARS

Parlor cars, offering first-class, daytime accommodations of plush, rotating seats in either a common area or in private rooms, comprised a relatively small percentage of Pullman's fleet. By 1930, at their height, there were 1,186 parlor cars on the Pullman roster. Their popularity waned during the Depression, though, and by 1947 there were only 231 parlor cars in Pullman service. Typically, parlor cars ran on lucrative, short-haul corridors where competing railroads maintained first-class service. The most common parlor routes were Washington, D.C.–New York–Boston, Chicago–St. Louis, Chicago–Twin Cities, and Chicago–Detroit.

For a short time following World War II, the parlor car enjoyed a resurgence of sorts, and New Haven briefly operated a streamlined version of the last all-parlor car train in the nation, the *Merchants Limited* from New York to Boston. Likewise, Pennsylvania Railroad introduced new streamlined parlor cars in 1952, on its streamlined *Senator* and *Congressional*. The Wabash even operated a new Pullman dome parlor car on its *Bluebird* between Chicago and St. Louis. Pullman parlor car service lasted until 1956 when the last users—PRR, Wabash, and NH—bowed out of Pullman service and began operating their own parlor car service.

One of the most popular trains in the country, Pennsylvania Railroad's *Broadway Limited*, remained an all-Pullman train until 1967. It is shown at Fort Wayne, Indiana, in 1966. *George Krambles, Krambles–Peterson Archive*

Among the most famous trains in the country and with a pedigree dating to the 1880s, Chicago & North Western's *North Western Limited* threads its way into Chicago's North Western Terminal in 1949. The train sports new streamlined Pullman cars in the *Northern* series. *C&NW photo*

The *Pioneer Limited* loads mail and express at Chicago Union Station prior to its late-evening departure for the Twin Cities in February 1968. At one time, Pullman's bread and butter had been overnight middle-distance trains such as this, but by 1968 the *Pioneer* was one of only a handful left. This evening, the train carries only two Pullman cars. *Bob Schmidt*

DINING AND RESTAURANT CARS

Pullman's original role in providing full dining service on the railroads' top trains started in the late 1800s, but by the 1920s, the practice had all but vanished as the railroads themselves increasingly offered full dining car services. Nevertheless, for a time Pullman maintained a small roster of diners to assist railroads afflicted with imbalanced seasonal movements. For example, the Atlantic Coast Line often used Pullman or other off-line diners to supplement its service when the Florida winter travel rush hit each December. In 1930, the Pullman roster included 18 dining cars.

A resurrection of Pullman dining service came in the early 1930s. The Depression had cut passenger train ridership by 40 percent nationally, and full diners weren't always necessary, especially on roads with moderate ridership, such as Wabash, Erie, Chicago Great Western, Kansas City Southern, Nickel Plate, Pere Marquette, Chesapeake & Ohio, and the Rock Island. Pullman stepped in to provide a less labor-intensive restaurant service focused on first-class passengers. The company offered a series of combination cars containing a mix of either sections and a restaurant, or parlor seats and a restaurant. It was a cost-effective way of replacing railroad-operated full dining service with a car's typical crew of four cooks, seven waiters, and a steward. Pullman provided service with a crew less than half that size. Between 1932 and 1939, Pullman rebuilt approximately 79 cars

Perhaps the most famous train in the country, the Santa Fe *Super Chief* was regularly scheduled as an all-Pullman train into the mid-1950s. Seasonally, the train ran as an all-Pullman operation during the summer peaks and winter holidays for most years thereafter. The all-Pullman section of the *Super Chief* is pictured at Los Angeles Union Passenger Terminal on December 22, 1968, just days before Pullman exited the U.S. railroad business for good. *Bob Schmidt*

Southern Pacific's crack all-Pullman overnight train between San Francisco and Los Angeles, the *Lark*, arrives in Glendale, California, in October 1953. *Donald Duke photo, courtesy of Tom Gildersleeve slide productions*

to provide restaurant service, and it rebuilt at least 2 other cars with buffet kitchens. These cars supplemented dozens of other existing cars built in 1929 and 1930 that provided either restaurant or buffet service in addition to either sleeping or parlor facilities.

Pullman's delectable meals were dispensed on daytime routes such as the Pere Marquette trains from Chicago to Grand Rapids. Overnight travelers also could enjoy Pullman fare aboard trains such as the *Nickel Plate Limited* from Chicago to Cleveland, the *Hustler* from New Orleans to Shreveport, or the *Erie*

Limited between New York and Chicago. While the service declined significantly after World War II, it was still possible to enjoy Pullman meals on the PRR between Washington and New York, on the southland, or on the *Bar Harbor Express* to Maine.

The last survivors offering some form of Pullman meal service in 1968 were the Pullman lounge on New Haven's *Federal*, where a club breakfast was available, and Union Pacific's *Butte Special*, where 2 converted sections of a 6-6-4 postwar-built *American* series sleeper turned out modest meals.

The last traditional streamliner built with Pullman cars was the *Denver Zephyr* of 1956. In this stunning view, the *DZ* is shown at Chicago in 1970. The rear of the train comprises a dome parlor-observation car and three former Pullman-operated sleepers, including a *Slumbercoach* with its distinctive staggered windows. *Bob Schmidt*

Burlington Northern train No. 1, *Denver Zephyr*, heads west at Harlem Avenue in Chicago in February 1971. The train's sleeping cars, including a high-density slumber coach, are in the foreground. *Bob Schmidt*

PRIVATE CARS FOR LEASE

Pullman also maintained a small fleet to cater to the needs of those who had the means to travel in private cars. Prior to the turn of the century, Pullman maintained a robust variety of private car types for charter, including hunting cars for parties touring the West. By the late 1920s, the majority of the 24 private cars available for lease on the Pullman roster had a configuration that was similar to a railroad office car with sleeping, dining, and lounge facilities,

and an open observation platform. Pullman's 1924 private car catalog did include one composite Baggage Club car, a parlor car, a few regular sleepers, and a tourist sleeper for railroads that wanted to assemble a train. The Pullman private car fleet numbered 34 cars in 1910, 24 cars in 1930, 17 cars in 1940, and just 2 cars by 1944. The opulent way of life symbolized by the Pullman private car was largely a thing of the past by the end of World War II.

Family members wave goodbye to relatives aboard the beautiful *Golden State* at Alhambra, California, in 1953. The train's Pullman sleeper-observation car is preceded by a 10-6 sleeper, a 4-4-2 sleeper, a diner, and two 6-6-4 sleepers. *Donald Duke photo, courtesy of Tom Gildersleeve slide productions*

THE WOOD-CAR ERA:

1867–1910

PULLMAN'S PALACE CAR COMPANY WAS INCORPORATED IN ILLINOIS IN 1867. At the time, the firm owned 48 sleeping cars and had negotiated contracts with the Chicago & Alton; Michigan Central; Chicago, Burlington & Quincy; Chicago Great Western; and the Great Western Railway of Canada. It soon added the Chicago & North Western (C&NW). Pullman introduced the hotel car in 1867, which was simply a sleeping car with a small kitchen. A year later, Pullman built *Delmonico*, the first full-service dining car complete with a kitchen and dining room.

The New York Central and Hudson River's *Fast Mail* is pictured running at track speed under High Bridge over the Harlem River circa 1901. The view epitomizes the American express train at the height of railroading's power and majesty, at the dawn of the new century. *Frank Willis Blauvelt, author collection*

Initially, Pullman's cars were built at the shops of various railroads and car-building firms. But as the company's business grew and with George Pullman's aspiration to build cars for others, Pullman acquired the Detroit Car & Manufacturing Company in 1870.

A decade later, George Pullman built a new car works 15 miles south of the company's Chicago headquarters near Lake Calumet, Illinois. Here he not only established state-of-the-art shops but also the model town of Pullman, Illinois, to house his workers. Pullman Car Works opened in 1881 and soon employed upwards of 2,000 people, many of them immigrant craftsmen drawn to the attractive homes they could rent and the town's modern schools, libraries, and parks. The Detroit facility was gradually converted from a car construction shop to a car repair shop.

As its operating territory expanded, the company added repair and remodeling shops at St. Louis,

Missouri (1880); Wilmington, Delaware (1886); Calumet, Illinois (1901); and Richmond, California (1901). With its acquisition of the Wagner Palace Car Company at the end of 1899, Pullman inherited that firm's car works at Buffalo, New York.

Early sleeping cars had often been staffed by employees of the railroad rather than the concessionaire. In some cases, passengers were expected to prepare their own berths. By 1870, George Pullman had concluded that he could control service standards only by staffing the cars with his own employees. For this, he drew extensively from the large pool of African Americans who had been emancipated by Abraham Lincoln. For the rest of its 100-year existence, Pullman exclusively employed black males in car porter positions. Beginning in 1925, Filipino men were added to the ranks of Pullman's dining, buffet, and lounge car attendants. The company's conductors were almost always white males.

33

The Pennsylvania Railroad's *Washington Limited* is shown at speed en route in 1896. *Frank Willis Blauvelt, author collection*

Pullman's preference was to have full control over as many aspects of the sleeping car business—car construction, ownership, maintenance, and staff—as possible. However, as an alternative to exclusive ownership of the cars and an effective method for getting a foothold with a prospective railroad client, Pullman sometimes entered into an association agreement with a railroad whereby the cars were jointly owned and maintenance costs and profits divided. This practice grew as the firm expanded its territorial reach through the 1880s, until nearly half of Pullman's fleet was owned via association agreements. As Pullman's fortunes improved or its railroad partners tired of the arrangement, the associations were dissolved. When that happened, Pullman generally acquired full ownership of the cars and contracted with the railroads to operate them. Most of the associations were terminated by the early 1900s, but the last—with the Spokane, Portland & Seattle Railway—survived until 1922.

CARS OF THE ERA

Pullman sleeping cars of the 1870s varied greatly in length but generally ranged between 60 and 66 feet over end sills, with an interior length of 54 to 60 feet. Common floor plans included 12 or 14 open sections with upper and lower berths, or 10 or 12 open sections and a private drawing room that enclosed a section and a sofa bed. Public lavatories were located at either end of the car. The women's facility was typically adjacent to the drawing room. Given that male passengers normally outnumbered women, the men's lavatory was generally the larger of the two. The car's smoking lounge, which also served as quarters for the car's porter, was adjacent to the men's lavatory—reflecting the social pressure against women smoking. By the end of the decade, it was standard practice to provide a private lavatory annex for the drawing-room passengers. A hotel sleeper incorporated a small buffet kitchen, sometimes in lieu of 2 sections or the drawing room. Initially illuminated by candles, oil lanterns came into widespread use for interior lighting by the end of the decade. The Baker Heater hot water system was widely used for heating.

Vancouver, constructed in August 1888, contained 12 sections, 1 drawing room, and a buffet. The car's elaborate exterior ornamentation was typical of Pullman cars built in the last decade of the nineteenth century. *Pullman photo*

Pullman added parlor cars to its fleet beginning in 1874. The company's business growing by leaps and bounds, Pullman now operated its cars between cities without regard to the territorial limits of individual railroads. The company's growing pool of cars proved to be a very efficient way to handle local surges in traffic. George Pullman's grand vision of a single enterprise providing a national pool of deluxe equipment along with a well-trained staff to maintain consistently high service standards for passenger comfort was taking form and would eventually distinguish Pullman from other sleeping car concessionaires of the period.

A passenger's expectations were met when he or she boarded a Pullman. Early Pullman palace cars introduced interior appointments intended to convey a sense of respectability, and established a baseline standard of luxury and comfort for a new, higher class of rail travel: first-class. Fine arts and services long associated with the possessions and pleasures of the wealthy were extended to the confines of a railroad car.

The interior decor of Pullman palace cars of the 1870s aimed for genteel elegance. Pullman cars of the 1880s, turned out by the company's own artisans at the new Pullman Car Works near Chicago, embraced even bolder and more ornate Victorian cabinet artistry and ornamentation. Be it richly upholstered furnishings, heavy velour draperies and silk fringes, patterned carpets, glass etchings, gilding, or fine marquetry (see sidebar, pages 38–40) and carvings in rare and beautifully finished woods, Pullman seemed determined to spare no expense. The investment in interior outfitting approached half of a new car's total expense. As the decade progressed, car exteriors also became more colorful, often painted in elaborate scrolling, striping, and lettering.

continued on page 41

The interior of Pullman diner *Alhambra* is shown in this Pullman image from 1888. The car was originally used on the Atlantic Coast Line's posh *New York and Florida Special*. In 1892, the car was sold to the Pennsylvania Railroad. *Pullman photo*

The Artistry of the Palace Car

A HINT OF THINGS TO COME ONCE INSIDE A PULLMAN PALACE CAR OF THE LATE NINETEENTH CENTURY was evident on the exterior, with the car's highly finished wood, painted and gilded with elaborate scrolls, striping, and lettering. Inside, travelers were awed by the opulence and extraordinary artistry on display, specifically the heavy rich fabrics, etched and beveled glass, brass ornamentations, wood carvings, and dark wood panels adorned with beautiful inlays of various designs.

Most striking was the marquetry—decorative work in which intricate patterns are formed by the insertion of pieces of wood or other material into a wood veneer that is then attached to a surface. The technique was initially employed by Pullman around 1876, in cars built at the company's Detroit Works, and continued in various forms through the wood-car era. Its practitioners were said to have been held in high esteem by George Pullman, himself a trained cabinetmaker. The most common application of marquetry was on upper-berth panels of rare wood such as mahogany and teak with elaborate inlays of geometric forms, flowers, fruits, or animals in the center, surrounded, at times, by delicate borders. Wood carving briefly replaced some marquetry during the mid-1890s but then faded from use. A form of berth marquetry survived for a while during the steel-car era through the artistry of the painter and finisher, but it eventually proved incompatible with Pullman's more modern interiors. Pullman marquetry was a labor-intensive and time-consuming task, requiring great artistry and care. Much of the work was entrusted to experienced craftsmen who emigrated from Europe.

As described in Pullman's in-house magazine, *The Pullman News*, "A stencil or pattern following the design was the first step, and it was made from strong bond paper, the holes being pricked with an ordinary sewing needle. This was mounted on a wooden frame and duplicates made on common white paper. The different parts of the design were carefully cut apart and each part pasted on a block of veneer consisting of seven layers of one-twentieth of an inch in thickness. These veneer blocks were cut out by a small jigsaw and every individual part was placed on a tray and carefully numbered. When all the small pieces comprising the marquetry design were cut, the whole stencil was pasted upon the main piece of veneer forming the large panel of a bunk or a partition. The panels were also fashioned in seven-ply and the outside line of the stencil was followed by the saw.

"The complete 7-plys [*sic*] of veneer were then separated and each of the seven panels was placed on a straight board where all of the different pieces were inlaid, and glued on paper to hold them in place. The reverse side of the panel was then inspected and any little crack or opening filled with an especially prepared putty. When this dried, the surface was scraped and then was ready to glue to the solid panel, which was constructed of five-ply solid lumber and veneer. After being dried for five or six days in a room heated to 100 degrees, the panel was ready to turn over to the Finishing Department."

Three coats of varnish were applied to the panels and rubbed with pumice stone and water before they were installed in a car.

"Although the rare woods used in marquetry furnished most of the shades needed for actual reproduction of nature's colors, there sometimes were exceptions when man's ingenuity had to step in. This was true of flowers and particularly in the shading of the edges of the leaf. Take the rose or a lily of the valley as examples. In the rose the satin veneer was used and the shading of the edges was obtained by placing minute pieces of the wood in hot sand. The heat burned the edges just enough to give the impression of the crumple and roll of a rose leaf. In the case of a red rose the veneer often was dyed the proper color. White holly veneer was generally used for dying purposes on account of its soft and even grain. This wood was used for the lily of the valley, and by shading the edges of the leaves in the hot sand a very

The interior of *Osiris*, an 1891 product of Pullman, was a masterpiece of the car builder's art. Inlaid and polished woods are seen in profusion, and the upper berth fronts above the seats are done in Pullman's "weeping willow" pattern. *Pullman photo*

close imitation of the flower was obtained, enough to please all flower lovers."

With the introduction of the all-steel car, metal interiors metamorphosed into mahogany, walnut, and oak at the hands of skilled and patient painters and finishers, as the *Pullman News* described. "Fifteen days are required to transform a steel bunk into a piece of mahogany. First the steel surface must be cleaned with benzene and emery cloth. Then it is sprayed by an air brush with the mahogany steel priming coat. The next day this has dried and lead putty is used to close any little holes in the surface. This is done with a knife, and if on the third day the surface is not smooth the operation is again performed. The fourth day finds the bunk being sandpapered down with emery cloth, and it is then sprayed with another coat of paint that forms the ground color, a dull red."

"Enter the grainer on the fifth day after another sandpapering. With a coating brush he applies a beautiful color composed of burnt Italian sienna, Van Dyke brown and French carmine. Then begins the woodcraft. With his small graining tool the expert carves out in the moist paint three hearts of wood. It is like studying a bisected tree, only in this instance one sees a human hand apparently doing in a few minutes what it takes Nature years to accomplish. It is a course grain, though, so the expert takes his mottler, a 3-inch flat brush with half-inch hairs, and begins to deftly cloud the surface. The resemblance grows but still there is something lacking. Ah, now it comes, the fine pores of the wood. He produces this effect with the blender, a heavier brush with badger hair, by stippling the surface."

Decorative striping and ornamentation is applied, followed by nine more days of repeated varnishing, drying, sandpapering, rubbing with pulverized pumice stone and water, and polishing before the job is complete.

Engravings from 1897 brochure advertising Grand Trunk Railway's Pullman service on the *Sea-Side* and *White Mountains Special*. *Author collection*

continued from page 36

The 1880s saw a general lengthening of sleeping cars by about 8 feet, permitting the addition of a pair of sections or larger lavatories, a smoking lounge, or a buffet. A new private accommodation, the stateroom, was included in some sleepers built toward the end of the decade. Frequently found in private rail car designs of the time, the stateroom enclosed a standard section and provided lavatory facilities. However, this accommodation was not widely used in Pullman's sleepers until early in the twentieth century, at which time it bore a new name: compartment.

This was also a period of major technological advances in passenger car safety and comfort. Pintsch gaslights, a development from Germany, gained favor over lanterns and remained a popular means of interior lighting until the second decade of the twentieth century. In addition, electric lighting was introduced on the Pennsylvania Railroad in 1882, and by 1887 a few trains were advertised as being entirely electric-lighted, generally from a steam-driven dynamo located in the baggage car. This not only improved lighting quality in a car but also reduced the risk of fire. It would be several decades, however, before electric lighting totally replaced gas. In addition, a practical way was found to efficiently use steam from the locomotive for car heating, hot water, and dining car steam tables. Air brakes were improved for greater safety and smoother train handling.

The introduction of the enclosed vestibule in 1887, however, had the greatest impact on the character and future of train travel. Based on an old concept but refined by H. H. Sessions, Pullman's superintendent of the Chicago Works, this narrow, accordion-like passageway, or diaphragm, between cars provided protection from the weather, minimized jarring, and reduced the danger of telescoping by

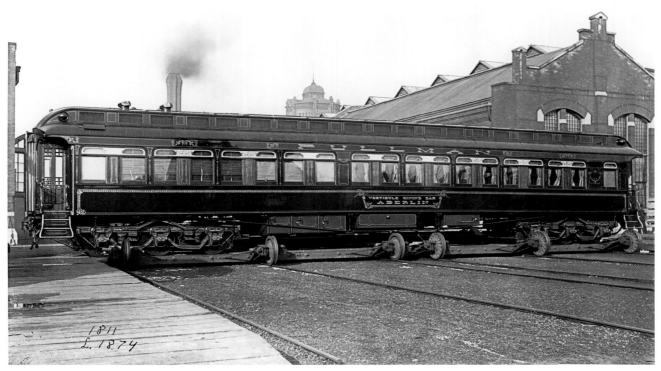

Aberlin was a Pullman narrow-vestibule diner turned out in 1892. Given a steel underframe and other upgrades, this car and another car, *Magdelin,* were sold to the Florida East Coast Railroad in 1920. Renamed *Alcazar* and *Ormond,* amazingly they remained in regular service until 1945. *Pullman photo*

keeping adjoining platforms horizontally aligned. No longer did a passenger feel confined to his or her car by the discomfort and risk associated with crossing between open platforms on a fast-moving train. While the hotel-style car had made it possible to endure a long trip without venturing into another car, now a passenger could move about the train freely, comfortably, and safely. This opened the way for railroads and concessionaires to offer a wide variety of services and amenities throughout the train. Of course, to get the full benefit of the enclosed vestibule, as well the recent advances in steam heat and electric lighting, it was necessary to use only cars so equipped in the train.

All-room sleeper *Superb*, out-shopped in November 1889, shows off its narrow vestibule and ornate paint finish on the Pullman transfer table before entering service. The car contained 6 drawing rooms. *Pullman photo*

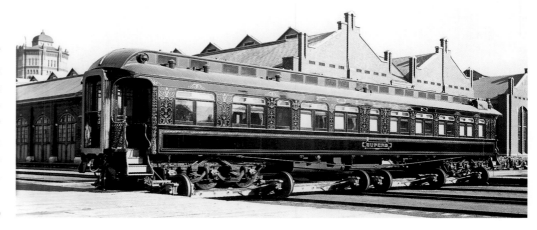

Banda, a 12-section, 1-drawing-room sleeper, was built in 1890. The car featured paper wheels and incredibly detailed fine lining on the trucks. *Pullman photo*

TRAINS OF THE ERA

Thus was born the "feature train" with its many on-board services. Dining, club, and observation cars; libraries and writing rooms; barber shops; shower baths; maid-manicurists; and stenographers were among the amenities found onboard these trains. Initially, a concessionaire such as Pullman provided most of these amenities, but as the railroads saw the self-promotional benefits of the feature train, they gave the trains colorful, often self-identifying or even grandiose names, and put their own brand on the services by owning and staffing the cars themselves. Promotional geniuses like New York Central's George H. Daniels were determined to differentiate the product (a specific train featuring deluxe accommodations and amenities) from the commodity (all passenger train schedules between points A and B) when challenging competitors in a particular market. And the principal beneficiary was the passenger.

The Pennsylvania Railroad's *New York & Chicago Limited*, introduced in 1881, was renamed the *Pennsylvania Limited* and inaugurated as the first all-Pullman vestibuled train in 1887. The next 20 years of unprecedented passenger-traffic growth, competition, and promotion saw the introduction of many of the vestibule trains that would remain household names well into the twentieth century. Among the most famous of the western transcontinental trains were the *Sunset Limited* (Southern Pacific; inaugurated in 1894); the *Overland Limited* (Union Pacific, Southern Pacific, and Chicago & North Western; 1896); the *California Limited* (Santa Fe; 1892); the *North Coast Limited* (Northern Pacific; 1900); the *Oriental Limited* (Great Northern Railway [GN]; 1905); and the *Golden State Limited* (Southern Pacific and Rock Island; 1902).

Notable overnight trains inaugurated in the East and Midwest during this period included the *Lake Shore Limited* (Commodore Vanderbilt's NYC System; 1897) and *South-Western Limited* (Commodore Vanderbilt's NYC System; 1889); *International Limited* (Grand Trunk Railway; 1900); *Fast Flying Virginian* (Chesapeake & Ohio; 1889); *Pioneer Limited* (Chicago, Milwaukee & St. Paul [CM&StP]; 1898); *North Western Limited* (Chicago & North Western; 1898); and *The Limited* (Chicago, Burlington & Quincy; 1897).

The *New York–Florida Special* (1888) on the Pennsylvania Railroad; Richmond, Fredericksburg & Potomac; Atlantic Coast Line; Plant System; and Florida East Coast; and the *Dixie Flyer* on the Nashville, Chattanooga & St. Louis (1892) brought feature train service to the South.

Section, drawing room, stateroom, sleeper *Spokane* was an 1890 product. The car was owned by the Pullman–Northern Pacific Association. *Pullman photo*

Osiris was a narrow-vestibule sleeper turned out in 1891. The car contained 12 sections and 1 drawing room, and was built to Pullman Plan 784. The ornate lettering is typical of the period. *Pullman photo*

Several East Coast daytime runs had deluxe parlor car operations. These runs included Lehigh Valley's *Black Diamond* (1896); New York Central's *Empire State Express* (1891); Pennsylvania Railroad's *Congressional Limited* (1882, vestibule equipped after 1887); New Haven's *Bay State Limited* (1893), *Gilt Edge* (1899), and *Merchants Limited* (1903); and Baltimore & Ohio's fleet of Royal Blue Line trains (1890), including the *Royal Limited* (1898). On the West Coast, Southern Pacific's deluxe *Del Monte* (1889) linked San Francisco and the Monterey Peninsula.

The Chicago & Alton Railroad operated two deluxe trains between Chicago and St. Louis with Pullman services, the *Alton Limited* on a daytime run and the overnight *Midnight Special*. Although these services began late in the wood-car era, the Alton's relationship with Pullman had its roots in the construction of Pullman and Benjamin C. Field's first

sleeper, No. 9, in 1859, and the introduction of the *Pioneer* car in 1865 and the *Delmonico* dining car in 1868. The *Alton Limited* was inaugurated in 1899 with new Pullman vestibule equipment. Known as the "red train" for its color, the luxurious consist included a Pullman buffet car and parlor-observation car. In time, the train became famous for its afternoon tea served by a Japanese maid. Illinois Central's two long-running trains, *Daylight Special* (1893) and *Night Diamond Special* (1891), operated in direct competition with the *Alton Limited* and *Midnight Special*.

The sleeping and parlor cars and sometimes the dining cars on many of the vestibuled feature trains of the period were owned and staffed by Pullman. However, a number of the railroads contracted with rival concessionaires, most notably the Wagner Palace Car Company for trains that operated within Commodore Vanderbilt's NYC System. Other roads,

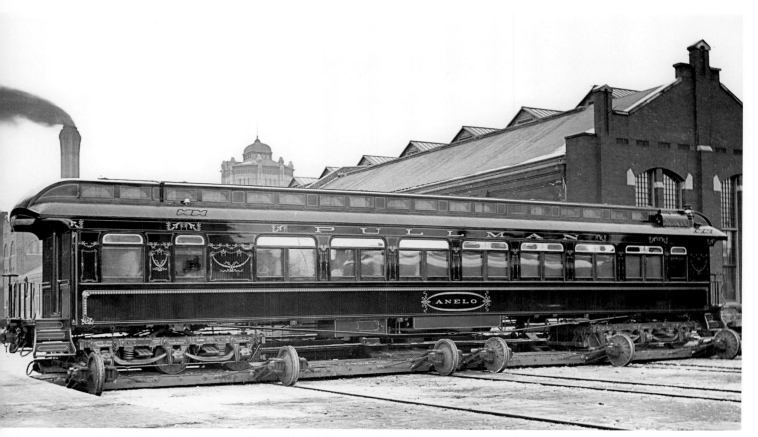

Anelo, a 14-section sleeper constructed in 1893 for general-service assignment; surprisingly, it had open platforms. *Pullman photo*

such as CM&StP, used their own cars and personnel. Occasionally, a railroad would have contracts with more than one concessionaire or would use a concessionaire's services along with its own equipment and staff.

A prime example of a train with sleeping car services provided by both Pullman and Wagner was the famous *Continental Limited*, linking Boston and New York City with the Midwest over lines of the Fitchburg (Boston–Albany), West Shore (Weehawken–Buffalo), and Wabash (Buffalo–Detroit–St. Louis–Kansas City–Council Bluffs–Des Moines) railroads. The *Official Guide of the Railways* (June 1898) lists the following sleeping car lines for the westbound train:

Wagner Palace Car sleeper: Boston to St. Louis
Wagner Palace Car sleeper: New York
    (Weehawken) to St. Louis

Wagner Palace Car sleeper: Buffalo to Detroit
Pullman Palace Car sleeper: St. Louis to
    Kansas City
Pullman Palace Car buffet-sleeper: St Louis to
    Council Bluffs
Pullman Palace Car buffet-sleeper: St. Louis to
    Minneapolis
Pullman Palace Car buffet-sleeper: Kansas City
    to Des Moines

Sleepers built in the 1890s tended to standardize on the 12-section, 1-drawing-room floor plan. The dark interior paints, finishes, and fabrics that had characterized the cars of the 1870s and 1880s gradually gave way to slightly lighter colors. There was greater emphasis on wood carving and somewhat less emphasis on fancy marquetry as interior appointments and decor became more conservative. This trend

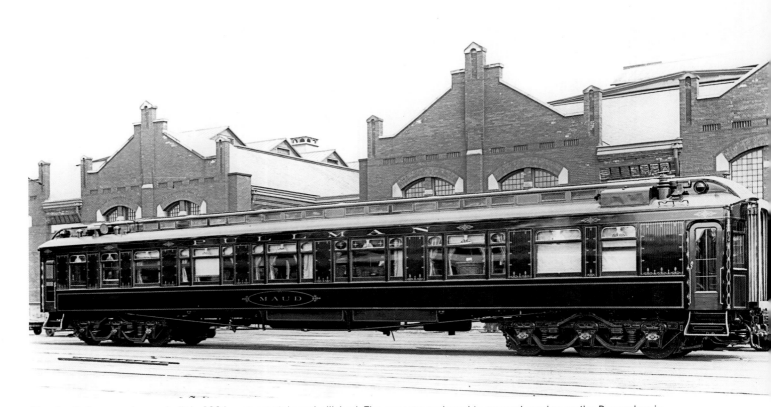

Maud, a Pullman parlor car built in 1894, was ornately embellished. The car was assigned to general service on the Pennsylvania Railroad. *Pullman photo*

The interior of the car *Maud* shows the lavish surroundings available to regular Pullman passengers in the 1890s. Note the brocade-covered chairs, the elaborate curtains, and the chipped-glass clerestory windows in the ceiling. *Pullman photo*

seemed to accelerate after Robert Todd Lincoln, first son of Abraham Lincoln, succeeded George Pullman as company president upon Pullman's death in 1897. The aggressive promotion of tourism, especially in the West, prompted the construction of high-capacity 14- and 16-section cars with even less ornamentation for this economy-minded clientele.

The 1890s also saw cars approach 80 feet in length, vestibules extended to the full width of the car, the substitution of tongue-and-groove exterior sheathing for panels, and some limited use of iron and steel reinforcement in car construction. Locomotive-supplied steam heat on feature trains also gained rapid acceptance. Car architecture underwent a modest refinement through the occasional use of oval, bay, and picture windows.

A number of other sleeping car concessionaires had developed and grown, and in a few cases given Pullman stiff competition. The Central Transportation Company (CTC), organized in 1862, was probably the largest and strongest competitor after the Civil War. CTC brought together the interests of T. T. Woodruff and Edward C. Knight. A subsidiary of CTC, the Southern Transportation Company, focused on sleeping car lines in the Southeast. CTC fielded a fleet of lavish *Silver Palace* cars. Pullman

leased CTC in 1870, thereby muting the competitive threat. In addition, Union Palace Car Company was formed in 1888. It was an evolution of the Crescent City Sleeping Car Company (Pullman Southern), Jonah Woodruff's Sleeping & Parlor Coach Company, Lucas Sleeping Car Company, and the Mann Boudoir Car Company. Pullman acquired Union Palace Car Company in 1889.

The most successful of Pullman's competitors was Webster Wagner's New York Central Sleeping Car Company (named the Wagner Palace Car Company in 1886). Wagner held contracts on most of the Vanderbilt-controlled railroads and was increasingly encroaching on former Pullman territory, such as the Michigan Central and Chicago & North Western.

Despite this spirited competition, plus the several railroads that chose to own and operate their own sleeping cars (notably the CM&StP, GN, and NH), Pullman dominated the market. Gradually, the firm drove out of business or bought out each concessionaire until only Wagner remained. Wagner was a formidable and contentious competitor, and was the last sleeping car concessionaire to capitulate to Pullman. It took a bitter legal dispute over patents and operating contracts to force Wagner to sell in late 1899.

Laconia, a 12-section, 1-drawing-room sleeping car, was constructed in 1898 for service on the Erie Railroad. The car contained the new oval-window design. *Pullman photo*

TURN OF THE CENTURY

In 1900, Pullman's Palace Car Company changed its name to The Pullman Company. George Pullman's marketing prowess, financial maneuvering, obsessive control, and self-promotion had propelled his company into a virtual monopoly position in the construction and operation of sleeping cars. The Pullman Company now hoped to enhance its fortunes by standardizing its equipment, services, and contractual relationships, even as the railroads were increasingly trying to define and promote their own brand through accommodations and services unique to their particular trains.

The 12-section, 1-drawing-room floor plan dominated the Pullman fleet. At least one 12-1 sleeper could be found in the consist of virtually every overnight train in the country during the first decade of the new century. However, the growth of travel by women and a boom in upscale vacation trips to southern climes in the winter and the West

in the summer boosted the demand for private room accommodations. The two-berth private compartment with its own lavatory facilities, which had seen only limited use by several concessionaires in the 1890s (when it was known as a stateroom), proved ideal for this traffic. When added to the floor plan of a sleeper, each compartment typically replaced 2 sections. Increasing the number of private rooms with their own lavatories (while at the same time cutting back the number of open sections) had the further benefit of reducing the amount of non-revenue space needed for the communal restrooms and smoking lounges. At the same time, there was growing pressure to enlarge the size of these facilities for women, including dressing rooms, as the number of women travelers increased.

Faster trains and numerous high-profile accidents in which passengers were crushed or burned to death in wooden cars put public pressure on the railroads and Pullman to use equipment built of iron

continued on page 52

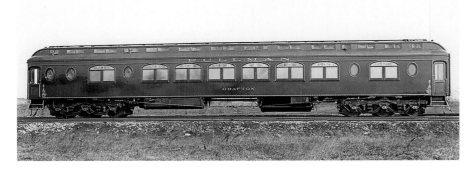

Grafton, a wood sleeper constructed in 1902, contained 12 sections and 1 drawing room. It was converted to a tourist car and placed in military service in May 1919, then converted back to a standard sleeper in December of the same year. The car was retired and destroyed by Pullman in 1926. *Pullman photo*

Pullman 8-section buffet lounge-observation car *Mound City* was a 1902 rebuild of the car *Puente* originally constructed in 1888. *Mound City* eventually became a Pullman supply and porter car in 1919. *Pullman photo*

The sections in the interior of *Mound City*, an 8-section buffet lounge-observation car are shown in this 1902 view. *Pullman photo*

Leipsic was originally an 1884-built, 10-section, 1-drawing-room sleeper owned by the Illinois Central. After IC joined Pullman in 1891, the car was eventually rebuilt circa 1903 into a 16-section sleeper, as shown here. *Pullman photo*

Asbury was a 12-section, 1-drawing-room sleeper delivered in October 1903 for service on the Illinois Central's *Night Diamond* between Chicago and St. Louis. *Pullman photo*

Brighton was one of 10 cars assigned to the Chicago, Alton & St. Louis in April 1905. It contained 16 open sections and a large smoking room/lavatory section. It was assigned to the railroad's *Midnight Special* between Chicago and St. Louis. *Pullman photo*

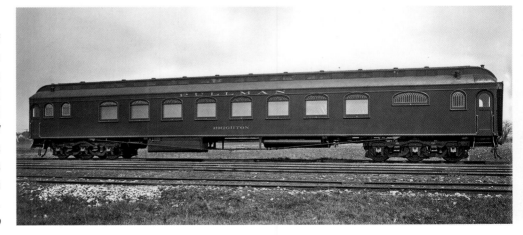

The interior of *Brighton* is shown looking through the smoking section of the car, toward the 16 open sections. *Pullman photo*

continued from page 48

or steel. At the same time, the trend toward longer and heavier passenger equipment was reaching the limit on the amount of strength that could be economically achieved in an all-wood car. A number of designs emerged for composite wood and steel cars. By the late 1890s and early 1900s, Pullman was installing steel platforms and end reinforcement in some of its wooden cars. In March 1907, the company completed its first all-steel car, the 12-section, 1-drawing-room *Jamestown*. The car was exhibited at the Master Carbuilders' Convention in Jamestown,

Virginia. Unfortunately, at 81 tons, the *Jamestown* was deemed too heavy. It would be three more years before Pullman had a 68-ton steel car prototype, the 12-1 *Carnegie*, ready for mass production. By the end of 1910, 300 steel cars had been built for use on the PRR through its new Hudson River tunnels entering New York City. Although the wood-car era officially ended in 1910, wooden sleepers could be found in rapidly declining numbers on Pullman rosters for several more decades.

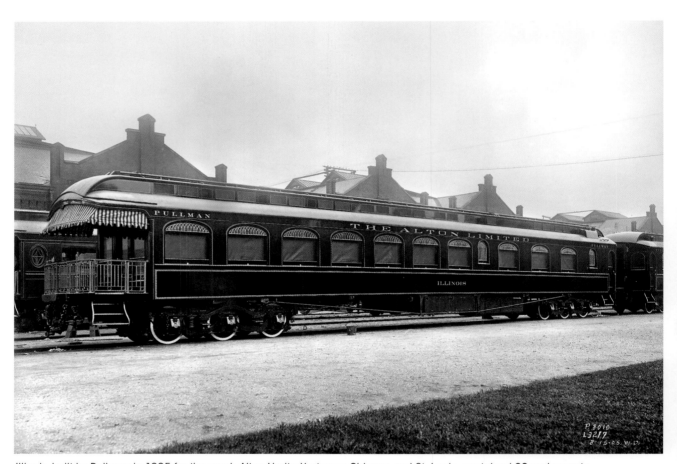

Illinois, built by Pullman in 1905 for the crack *Alton Limited* between Chicago and St. Louis, contained 20 parlor seats, 4 observation seats, a small buffet, and a 10-seat smoking room. Note the striped awning and white-walled wheels. *Pullman photo*

The interior of parlor-observation car *Illinois* was bright and cheery thanks to the lack of heavy curtains and the ample light coming in from the glass clerestory. The view looks rearward, past some of the car's swiveling parlor chairs toward the observation platform. *Pullman photo*

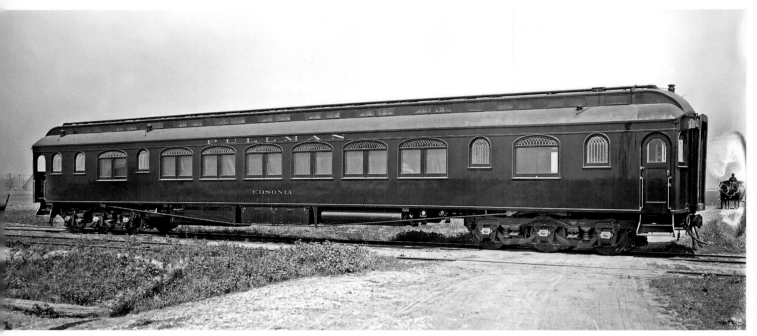

Edsonia was a 12-section, 1-drawing-room sleeper built in 1906. The car was assigned to the Chicago & Alton's Chicago–St. Louis run. *Pullman photo*

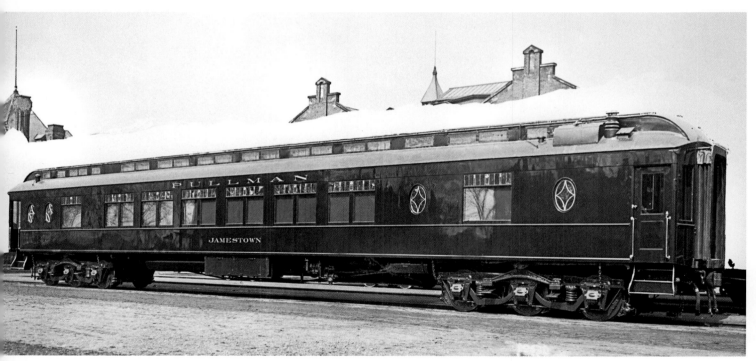

Seen here in a photo that was opaqued by someone in Pullman's ad department, *Jamestown* was Pullman's first all-steel sleeping car. The car met a growing desire to build fireproof and stronger rolling stock. The movement was hastened by railroads such as the Pennsylvania, which was building an entrance into New York City via newly built tunnels and thus insisted on steel equipment. *Pullman photo*

The interior of the 12-section, 1-drawing-room car *Jamestown*, built in 1907, was finished in light colors, uncharacteristic for

Among the many details of a turn-of-the-century Pullman car was this wood-grain interior in the 10-section, 1-drawing-room, 2-compartment sleeper *Laguna*, out-shopped in April 1906 for general service. *Pullman photo*

Carnegie, built in 1910, was Pullman's first production steel car. It was part of a large group of steel cars built by Pullman for assignment to the Pennsylvania Railroad that year. The creation of Pennsylvania Railroad's grand new terminal in Manhattan, reached by tunnels, motivated the giant railroad to require the use of steel cars for safety. *Pullman photo*

The steel framing for the *Carnegie* is shown to good advantage in this view taken at the Pullman plant. *Pullman photo*

A turn-of-the-century brochure touts Pullman accommodations on the Burlington Route's Chicago–Denver "Number One." *Author collection*

THE exterior of the train is uniformly
of the familiar Pullman color. It is
made up of Sleeping cars, Reclining
Chair cars, a Buffet Observation Smoking
car, and a Dining car in which the service
is à la carte. Between cars are wide
vestibules built of steel and beveled plate
glass.

THE STANDARD STEEL-CAR ERA:
1910–1932

3

LESS THAN A DECADE INTO THE TWENTIETH CENTURY, as Pullman was ascending to the pinnacle of its success, the company underwent a radical shift in the way it handled its passengers. For decades, the wooden railroad car had been the standard of American passenger carriage, but the world was changing. New York's pioneering Interborough Rapid Transit cars of the early 1900s had a steel construction to reduce the risk of fire. Fires within tunnels were of particular concern. Interborough's neighbor, the giant Pennsylvania Railroad, had been tunneling under the Hudson River on an ambitious project to put a passenger station in the heart of Manhattan and likewise was focused on developing steel rolling stock. Other railroads took notice.

The Baltimore & Ohio's *Shenandoah* curves away from the camera in this view. *Jonathan Club,* a buffet lounge–sunroom car with 8 sleeper sections brings up the rear of the attractive train. The train is shown on the eastern slope of the Allegheny Mountains. *Bill Price, Harry Stegmaier collection*

By 1906, Pullman management decided to proceed with the development of steel cars. Pullman completed its first experimental steel car, the 12-section, 1-drawing-room sleeper *Jamestown*, in March 1907. Well built but very heavy at 81 tons, the *Jamestown* contributed to Pullman's efforts to perfect the steel car. A second prototype, the 12-section, 1-drawing-room sleeper *Carnegie*—built for assignment to the PRR—was completed in 1910. Weighing in at 68 ½ tons, the *Carnegie* solved the weight problem while proving durable and safe. From then on Pullman never looked back. It committed to the massive undertaking of converting to steel cars completely, and no new wooden Pullman cars were built after 1910. By 1913, 2,100 all-steel sleeping cars (one-third of Pullman's fleet) were in operation. An additional

600 wooden cars had been converted to include all-steel underframes.

Standardization was key to Pullman's car-building and operating philosophy, and it was the hallmark of the heavyweight era for the company's manufacturing arm. The radical change to steel-car construction was virtually a new beginning, allowing Pullman to start fresh. The manufacturing company used identical car shells, trucks, and other parts for hundreds of cars despite their differences in final floor plan and window arrangement.

The Pullman operating company standardized by focusing on the open section as its primary accommodation. Pullman would eventually field more than 100 car floor plans and 457 subclasses of floor plans in its fleet. Half of the approximately 8,000 cars it built

P. 37187. C. S.
WILLIAM WYATT BIBB.
PLAN. 3411.
4-8-32. P.V.V.

Above: A Pullman open section arranged for daytime use. Lower-berth passengers rode facing forward. Upper-berth passengers—who paid less—rode facing backwards. Often, two total strangers would ride in this accommodation. *Pullman photo, courtesy Bob's Photo*

Left: For decades, the traditional scene that greeted Pullman passengers was this walk down an aisle of open-section accommodations. This view shows the interior of the *William Wyatt Bibb*, a 10-section, 3-double-bedroom rebuild for the Southern Railway's *Crescent Limited*. *Pullman photo, courtesy Bob's Photo*

A lower berth in a section made up for nighttime occupancy. Note the thick mattress across both berth seats, the netting for belongings, and the heavy berth curtains with the section number prominently displayed to prevent confusion when returning to one's section in the middle of the night. In the days before air-conditioning, porters often stretched an extra sheet across the open window to keep out dust and cinders at night. *SP photo*

and operated between 1910 and 1935 were 12-section, 1-drawing-room cars. By 1931, 4,000 12-1 cars were on the Pullman roster, comprising roughly 40 percent of the Pullman car fleet. Most were built to Plan 2410, or later to Plan 3410, which was introduced in 1923.

As Pullman's business grew over the first two decades of the twentieth century, so did the size and complexity of its fleet. Catering to the whim of first-class passengers seeking relief from the tedium of three-, two-, and even just one-day journeys, Pullman operated a group of lounge cars on top trains. The Baggage Club car debuted in the steel-car era in 1910 with a series of cars assigned to the PRR. Numerous others arrived in the next two decades. They were found operating on top trains such as New York Central's *20th Century Limited* and Pennsylvania Railroad's *Broadway Limited* (both New York–Chicago), and on Southern Railway's *Crescent Limited*

continued on page 68

Diversions were available in the solarium lounge of the *Empire Builder* between Chicago and the Pacific Northwest via Montana. This photo dates to 1929 or 1930. *GN photo, courtesy Bob's Photo*

Building a Heavyweight Pullman

**THE PULLMAN COMPANY'S DOMINATION OF OVERNIGHT RAIL-
ROAD TRAVEL** in the first half of the twentieth century
encompassed every aspect of the American sleeping car industry—from design and construction of
the cars and their specialized components to maintenance, onboard and administrative staffing, accounting, and advertising. Following the change to
steel cars initiated in 1907, the Pullman fleet assumed
an outward uniformity that masked the myriad variations within different series of dark green sleeping cars.
As master of its domain—at least until federal antitrust
action launched in 1940 ended Pullman's virtual monopoly over sleeping car construction and operation
in the United States—most of Pullman's standard-era
steel sleeping cars were built by the company's car-
building arm at its vast works south of Chicago. As an
industrial example of vertical integration surpassed
only by Henry Ford's River Rouge complex near Detroit (where raw iron ore went in one end and finished
automobiles came out the other), the paternal company town of Pullman, Illinois, housed thousands of
workers, administrators, and their families in a tightly
controlled residential hierarchy under the omnipres-
ent (and omnipotent) shadow of a sprawling manufacturing and assembly complex.

Just exactly how did the Pullman Car & Manufacturing Company go about building a heavyweight
steel sleeping car? Thanks to *The Story of the Pullman Car* by Joseph Husband (published in 1917 by
the A. C. McClurg Company of Chicago under Pullman Company auspices), it's possible to follow the
process that was repeated, thousands of times, over
the course of more than two decades.

Embarking on his tour of the Pullman Works, Husband encountered the structural core of several yet-
to-be-built sleeping cars. "At one side of one of the
main aisles a half-dozen great steel girders, like keels
for giant ships, lie on the floor. These are the mighty
box girders, 81 feet in length and weighing over 9 tons

each, which will form the backbone of future Pullmans.
To each of these girders, or sills, are riveted plates, an-
gles, and steel castings which extend the full length
of the car and platforms, as well as floor beams, cross
bearers, bolsters, and end sills of pressed steel. On
this foundation the side sills are riveted, steel beams
that run the entire length of the car.

"When this gray mass of steel is finally riveted
together with its cover plates, tie plates, and floor
plates," Husband continued, "the underframe of the
car is completed—an almost indestructible foundation which alone weighs 27,365 pounds. On this underframe the superstructure or frame is erected to
form the body of the car. This frame is composed of
pressed steel posts and plates, forming for each side
a complete girder, which would by itself alone carry
the entire weight of the loaded car.

"The roof deck is separately assembled, and as
soon as the superstructure of the car is ready it [the
roof] is swung up by a crane and dropped into place.
Like the rest of the car, the roof is of steel, braced
and riveted to defy the greatest possible strains.
The ends and vestibules are now built on, piece by
piece, until the skeleton of the car is complete. The
vestibules are particularly imposing, for on each side,
framing the side doors through which the passengers
enter the car, are giant beams of steel so built into
the construction of the frame that only under most
extraordinary circumstances could the force of a
collision crush the vestibule or the car behind it.

"The trucks . . . are marvels of strength and efficiency. Each of the two trucks has six steel wheels
weighing 900 pounds apiece. Added to this is the
weight of the three 600-pound axles, the two steel
castings which form the framework for the trucks
together with the bolsters, springs, equalizers, and
brake equipment—a total weight of 42,000 pounds
for the trucks alone, contributed to the total weight
of the car.

Minutes into its journey from San Francisco to New Orleans, the *Sunset Limited* pauses at Burlingame, California, in 1924. The train is the epitome of the heavyweight first-class trains and is largely made up of Pullman cars, except for Southern Pacific diner and head end cars. Riding the back platform was a time-honored tradition in the standard era. *SP photo*

"The car is now subjected to a thorough sand-blasting, a process that removes every particle of scale, grease, or dirt and leaves the steel in perfect condition to receive the first coat of paint and the insulation. To the passenger, the presence of the steel construction is apparent, but the insulation, which forms a vital factor in the car's construction, can be seen only during the process of building. Composed of a combination of cement, hair, and asbestos, this insulating material is packed into every cubic inch of space between the inner and outer shells of the roof and sides, forming a perfect non-conductor to protect the passengers against the biting cold of winter or the heat of summer sunshine. A similar cement preparation is next laid on the floor, combining the quality of a non-conductor of heat and cold with sanitary qualities invaluable as an aid in maintaining the cars in a strictly sanitary condition.

"At this point in the construction the car is turned over to the steamfitters, plumbers, and electricians. To see the Pullman car at this stage is to see a network of steam pipes and electric conduit lacing in and out between the gaunt steel frame of the car, and everywhere the white plaster-like insulation packed into every cavity. As soon as these gangs of workmen have finished, other workers fit into place the interior panel plates, partitions, lockers, and seat frames, and the car instantly assumes a new and almost completed aspect. Meanwhile, the painters have completed their work on the exterior of the car and begin the finer finish of the interior. Here coat upon coat is laid, and after each coat laborious rubbing to give the required finish. The graining, by which various woods are so faithfully imitated, is then applied, and last the varnishing."

This latter paint treatment was an art form in itself, simulating the appearance of wood grain on panels and trim in all-steel cars where, as Husband declared, "One man can trundle in a single wheelbarrow all the wood that has gone into its construction."

Installation of any remaining small fixtures, as well as curtains, window shades, carpeting, seat cushions, upholstery, mattresses, and linens completed the construction and assembly process, with the car now ready to join its fleet mates out on the road.

continued from page 64

(New York–New Orleans) and Seaboard Air Line's seasonal *Orange Blossom Special* (New York–Miami). Often these cars had a buffet and a shower facility, the latter usually the only bathing facility onboard. These cars were usually a male bastion. They often contained a barbershop, where a Pullman barber would care for first-class customers. In addition, the barber would frequently dispense valet services. Here amidst a haze of tobacco smoke one might encounter boxer Gene Tunney on the *Crescent* on his way to a prize fight, financial genius Clarence Barron of *Barron's* magazine on the *Century*, or a well-known senator heading back home to his district on the Baltimore & Ohio's Washington–Chicago *Capitol Limited*. Pullman dormitory lounges served mid-train on

the Union Pacific/Southern Pacific's famous *Overland Limited* and Rock Island's *Golden State Limited* (Chicago–Los Angeles), beginning in the 1920s.

While lounges operated on the top trains, the most common heavyweight Pullman cars were those with a mixture of sections and enclosed rooms to serve more than one passenger. Pullman eventually fielded 26 different car types, which included a mix of sections and other accommodations. Among the most prevalent, the company introduced the 10-section, 1-drawing-room, 2-compartment sleeper between 1911 and 1927. This floor plan, which squeezed more premium rooms into the car by eliminating two sections and having smaller communal washrooms than a 12-1, operated nationwide and comprised a large

continued on page 72

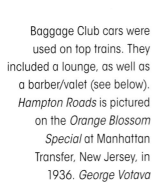

Baggage Club cars were used on top trains. They included a lounge, as well as a barber/valet (see below). *Hampton Roads* is pictured on the *Orange Blossom Special* at Manhattan Transfer, New Jersey, in 1936. *George Votava*

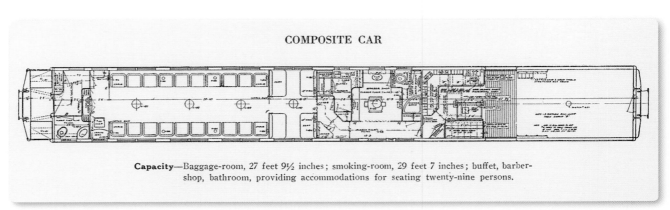

COMPOSITE CAR

Capacity—Baggage-room, 27 feet 9½ inches; smoking-room, 29 feet 7 inches; buffet, barbershop, bathroom, providing accommodations for seating twenty-nine persons.

68   CHAPTER 3

Crystal Bluff was a 3-compartment, 2-drawing-room, observation–lounge car assigned to the Santa Fe. Similar cars were assigned to the Southern Pacific/Rock Island *Golden State Limited* and the Union Pacific/Southern Pacific *San Francisco Overland Limited*. *Pullman photo, Krambles–Peterson Archive*

Theolinda was a 26-seat, heavyweight parlor car (see below) that also offered a drawing room. It was built to Pullman Plan 2416, a very common parlor car type in the Pullman fleet. The car is pictured at North Adams, Massachusetts, in 1937. *Bob's Photo*

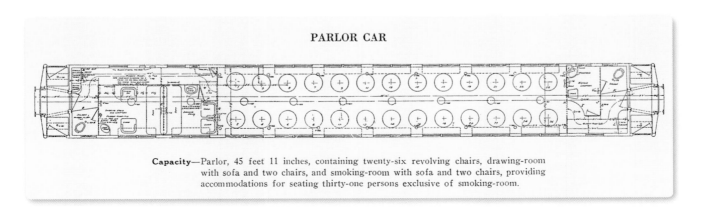

PARLOR CAR

Capacity—Parlor, 45 feet 11 inches, containing twenty-six revolving chairs, drawing-room with sofa and two chairs, and smoking-room with sofa and two chairs, providing accommodations for seating thirty-one persons exclusive of smoking-room.

The *San Francisco Overland Limited* is pictured on the Chicago & North Western at Geneva, Illinois, in 1934. A *Crystal*-series observation car is on the rear carrying the train's name proudly on a drumhead. *A. W. Johnson, Krambles–Peterson Archive*

Overland Limited

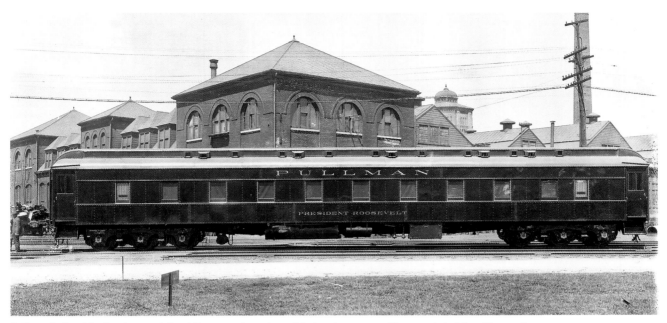

Pullman's *President* series contained 7 compartments and 2 drawing rooms. They predated the *Glen*-series cars. *Pullman photo, Krambles–Peterson Archive*

Glen Arden was one of a series of Pullman cars containing 6 compartments and 3 drawing rooms. Offering Pullman's most expensive heavyweight-era accommodations, they often held down assignments on top trains. *George Votava*

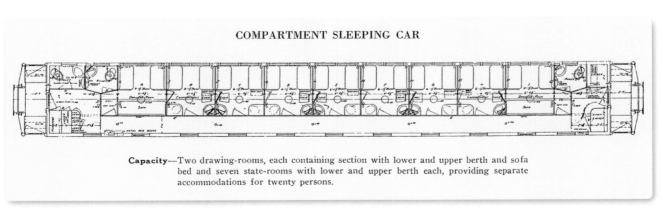

COMPARTMENT SLEEPING CAR

Capacity—Two drawing-rooms, each containing section with lower and upper berth and sofa bed and seven state-rooms with lower and upper berth each, providing separate accommodations for twenty persons.

continued from page 68

group of cars. Earlier cars of this type built before 1923 were constructed to Pullman Plan 2585. Cars with this floor plan, which began arriving in 1923, were built to Plan 3585 and primarily named in the *Lake* series.

Hundreds of all-section cars were introduced in the years before that accommodation began to fall from favor with the public. Pullman eventually fielded eight types of cars carrying nothing but sections. Between 1910 and 1920, Pullman introduced a large number of cars built to Plan 2412 with 16 sections. Almost all were eventually rebuilt to a different floor plan or converted to tourist cars. Between September 1925 and July 1930, Pullman put the Plan 3958,

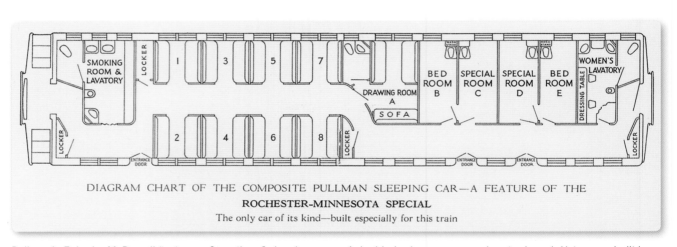

DIAGRAM CHART OF THE COMPOSITE PULLMAN SLEEPING CAR—A FEATURE OF THE
ROCHESTER-MINNESOTA SPECIAL
The only car of its kind—built especially for this train

Pullman's *Ephraim McDowell* (top)—an 8-section, 1-drawing-room, 4-double-bedroom car—and mate *Joseph Lister* were built in 1930 and assigned to Chicago & North Western, where they operated out of Chicago on the *Rochester–Minnesota Special* (above). In order to accommodate patients traveling to the Mayo Clinic, the cars were equipped with side doors for stretchers. *Pullman photo P35400, California State Railroad Museum*

Yosemite Park was a 4-compartment, 4-drawing-room Pullman car especially chartered by Raymond–Whitcomb Land Cruises, purveyors of fine travel out West. *Pullman photo, W. F. Stauss collection*

14-section sleeper in service on many top trains, including New York Central's *20th Century Limited*, Illinois Central's *Panama Limited*, Pennsylvania Railroad's *Broadway Limited*, Baltimore & Ohio's *Capitol Limited*, and Great Northern's *Empire Builder*. Interestingly, unlike the 16-section cars, most of the 14-section tourist cars Pullman created later were from other floor plans, such as the 12-1, and were not rebuilt from the original 14-section standard cars.

The all-private-room sleeping cars were a complete contrast to the proletarian all-section cars. Most of the all-private-room sleepers had a combination of drawing rooms and compartments. These aristocrats were typically used on top trains such as Santa Fe Railway's *Chief*; Chicago & North Western/Union Pacific/Southern Pacific *San Francisco Overland Limited*; Pennsylvania Railroad's *Broadway Limited* (cars named in the *Square* series); and several others. The most common of these were the 6-compartment, 3-drawing-room cars built to Plan 3523. Introduced between 1923 and 1930, the early cars of this series were named for great writers, composers, and artists. Later, cars in the group were typically, but not always, named in the *Glen* series. The 6-3 cars did double duty as they were also assigned in great numbers to the top winter-season-only Florida trains such as Atlantic Coast Line's *Florida Special* and Seaboard Air Line's *Orange Blossom Special*. Indeed, *Glen* cars could often be found in the *Florida Special* as late as the early 1960s. Their popular floor plan also made them valuable members of Pullman's roving pool of cars.

The 7-compartment, 2-drawing-room cars in Pullman Plan 2522 were lesser known. The class was originally introduced in 1910. Beginning in 1911, other early 7-2 cars were assigned to Santa Fe's top trains, the *California Limited* and exotic *de Luxe*. The last of the 7-2 cars were delivered in 1923 and named in the *President* series.

Tioga Valley carries the drumhead of the *20th Century Limited* at Harmon, New York, on May 30, 1938. Two weeks later the *Century* was re-equipped as a streamliner, and scenes like this of the train in its standard-era glory became memories. *George Votava, Bob's Photo*

In one of the great photos of the heavyweight era, the New York Central's *20th Century Limited* rolls out of Chicago eastbound for New York in January 1930. A Pullman baggage-club car is immediately behind the Hudson-type steam locomotive.
A. W. Johnson, Krambles–Peterson Archive

Twentieth Century Limited

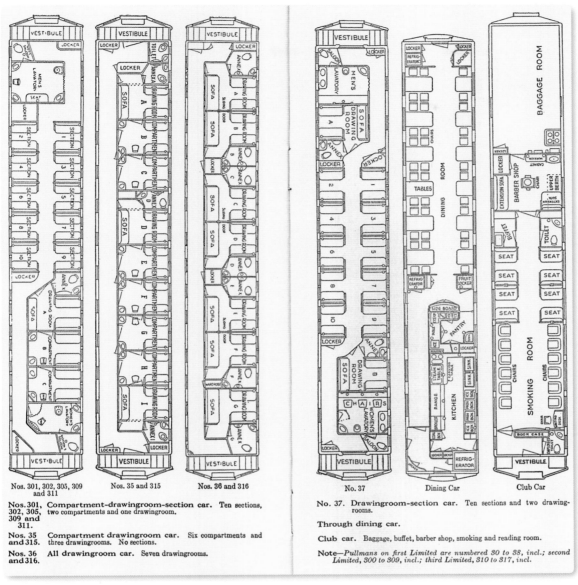

| Nos. 301, 302, 305, 309 and 311 | Nos. 35 and 315 | Nos. 36 and 316 | | No. 37 | Dining Car | Club Car |

Nos. 301, 302, 305, 309 and 311. Compartment-drawingroom-section car. Ten sections, two compartments and one drawingroom.

Nos. 35 and 315. Compartment drawingroom car. Six compartments and three drawingrooms. No sections.

Nos. 36 and 316. All drawingroom car. Seven drawingrooms.

No. 37. Drawingroom-section car. Ten sections and two drawing-rooms.

Through dining car.

Club car. Baggage, buffet, barber shop, smoking and reading room.

Note—*Pullmans on first Limited are numbered 30 to 38, incl.; second Limited, 300 to 309, incl.; third Limited, 310 to 317, incl.*

Cars in the *Willow* series contained 7 drawing rooms. They were assigned to top trains such as the Santa Fe's *California Limited* and the New York Central's *20th Century Limited. B. H. Nichols, author collection*

All-room cars with 7 drawing rooms built to Pullman Plan 2583 first appeared in 1911. They were assigned to the *de Luxe* and shortly thereafter to the *California Limited*. Twenty-five other cars built to Pullman Plan 3583 arrived between 1924 and 1929, named in the *Willow* series. These cars offered Pullman's most expensive accommodation at the time, and they typically were assigned to two of the top trains in the country, New York Central's *20th Century Limited* (New York–Chicago) and Santa Fe's *California Limited* (Chicago–California).

Cars that carried a mix of sleeping and lounge facilities and designed for mid-train use without an observation platform debuted in August 1927 with the arrival of the *Captain* and *Commander* cars. The 6-double-bedroom, café lounge cars built to Plan

Pullman's parlor buffet–dinette lounge the *Mask and Wig Club* was built in 1930 for assignment to the Pennsylvania Railroad. It is shown at Manhattan Transfer, New Jersey, on December 26, 1936. *George Votava, Bob's Photo*

Pullman rebuilt the *Old Elm Club* to Plan 4026 in December 1932. It was previously *Miloma*. The *Old Elm Club* contained 8 sections, 2 compartments, and a restaurant section. It was assigned to Chicago Great Western. *Pullman photo P34487 Krambles–Peterson Archive*

3974 were assigned to the Chicago & Alton's *Night Hawk* between St. Louis and Kansas City. In 1927, Plan 3975 debuted. This group comprised cars with a buffet lounge, an enclosed sunroom, a varying number of compartments, and one drawing room. Cars with 2 compartments, named in the *Sun* series such as *Sunbeam* and *Sunburst*, appeared on Missouri Pacific's *Sunshine Special*, while rival Katy Railroad's

Texas Special received cars named in the *Texas* series, such as *Texas Ranger*.

The most common variant of Plan 3975 was the 3-compartment, 1-drawing-room, buffet lounge, and enclosed sunroom car. This type appeared on Baltimore & Ohio's famous *Capitol Limited*, Union Pacific's *Pacific Limited*, and other trains, such as those operating from the Midwest to Florida. Similar to

Chicago Great Western train *The Minnesotan* crosses the Fox River at St. Charles, Illinois, in August 1934. The five-car train includes a Pullman restaurant-sleeper on the rear. *A. W. Johnson, Krambles–Peterson Archive*

West Virginia, a 1932 Pullman rebuild, contained 10 parlor seats and a restaurant lounge. It was assigned to the Chesapeake & Ohio. Note the Pullman "Indian Tree" china. *Pullman photo, Bob's Photo*

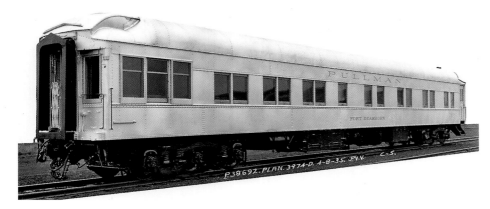

By the time the *Fort Dearborn* received its special aluminum paint, the car had been rebuilt to include 6 single bedrooms and 2 double bedrooms, as well as an observation lounge. It was assigned for years to Chicago & North Western's *North Western Limited*. *Pullman photo, courtesy Bob's Photo*

Many Pullman cars were sold to the railroads and released back to Pullman postwar. Atlantic Coast Line owned *Charles E. Perkins*, a 1930 Pullman product acquired by ACL in 1948. It contained 8 sections, 1 drawing room, and 2 compartments. *W. B. Cox, Krambles–Peterson Archive*

the sunroom lounge cars, 44 cars built to Plan 3989 arrived between 1929 and 1931. They all contained a mix of 8 sleeping sections and a buffet lounge. Named in the *Club* series, this type had nationwide assignment, operating from Maine to California.

In addition to mid-train lounge cars, the Pullman sleeper-observation lounge car was common in the 1920s. Observation cars operated on the rear of numerous trains and were usually equipped with a brass rail porch. From this vantage point, seated in a folding chair the intrepid traveler could observe the route recede behind him or her. Early examples of the sleeper-observation cars in the steel-car era include a series of cars with 6 compartments and an observation lounge built for assignment to the PRR in 1910, as well as cars with 8 compartments and an observation lounge built for New York Central's *20th Century Limited*. Beginning in 1911, a series of cars with 10 sections and an observation lounge were built to Plan 2521. Cars of this type were assigned to trains such as UP's *Overland Limited* between San Francisco and Chicago, the Santa Fe's *California Limited* between Los Angeles and Chicago, and the Louisville & Nashville Railroad's (L&N) *Pan American* between Cincinnati and New Orleans.

In the standard-car era, the 3-compartment, 2-drawing-room car with an observation lounge was among the most common sleeper-observation cars. They were built to Pullman Plan 3959. Delivered between 1925 and 1929, these 3-2 cars operated nationwide on many of the country's top trains, including the Santa Fe's famous *Chief*, the Southern Pacific's *Shasta Limited*, and Southern Railway's *Crescent Limited*.

Pullman parlor cars, cousins to the sleeping car, were significantly rarer than their sleeping car fleet mates. In 1930, for example, Pullman rostered approximately 8,000 sleeping cars and fielded about 1,100 parlor cars. The latter were used to provide first-class service on daytime runs and spent most of their time on a few select routes, usually operating between major cities. Washington–New York–Boston and Chicago–St. Louis were some of the more important routes that used parlor cars. New Haven's *Merchants Limited* and *Yankee Clipper* were among the famous trains that offered parlor cars. Both operated between New York and Boston. PRR employed a mammoth parlor fleet that primarily operated in dozens of trains plying the route between Washington, Philadelphia, and New York. Its most famous day train on the route was the *Congressional Limited*.

An experimental Pullman car, the high-density *Coach-Sleeper*, contained 45 beds. It was never successful. *Pullman photo, Bob's Photo*

A view of the interior of Pullman parlor car *Waterville*. The car was originally built in 1916 for assignment on the New Haven Railroad's *Merchants Limited*. Twelve parlor chairs and its drawing room were removed when it was rebuilt in 1933, leaving the car as a 20-seat parlor car with a buffet lounge, as shown here. *Pullman photo, courtesy Bob's Photo.*

The most numerous parlor cars had a floor plan that primarily offered individual parlor chairs. Some also contained an enclosed day drawing room with a couch and chair so larger parties could travel in privacy. Pullman parlor seating also was offered in a number of other types of mixed-use cars. During the standard-car era, Pullman operated 15 types of combination parlor-lounge cars. Likewise, the company eventually fielded a total of 15 different kinds of parlor-observation cars, combining parlor seating and a lounge. In addition to being assigned to the top parlor car trains such as the *Merchants Limited* and the *Congressional Limited*, parlor-observation cars could be found on the rear of trains such as the *Empire State Express* and *Twilight Limited* (NYC), the *Black Diamond* (Lehigh Valley), the *Banner Limited* (Wabash), and the *Pan American* (L&N).

Pullman's original role in providing full dining service on the railroads' top trains started in the late 1800s, but by the 1920s the practice had all but vanished as the railroads increasingly offered their own dining car services. Nevertheless, for a time Pullman maintained a small roster of diners to assist railroads burdened with imbalanced seasonal movements. This included Atlantic Coast Line, which often used Pullman or other off-line diners to supplement its service when the Florida winter travel rush hit in December each year. In 1930, for example, the Pullman roster included 18 full dining cars.

In its heyday, Pullman also maintained a small fleet to cater to the needs of those who had the means to travel in private cars. Prior to the turn of the century, Pullman maintained a robust variety of private car types for charter, including hunting cars for parties

Pullman-owned observation car *Crystal Point* was painted for *Olympian Hiawatha* service, as Pullman couldn't deliver the new train's lightweight sleepers in time for its inaugural. The car is shown on the rear of the train in June 1947 on the occasion of the *Olympian Hi*'s first westbound trip. *Russell Luedke, W. F. Stauss collection*

Sleeper *Red Rock Pass* contained 8 sections, 1 drawing room, and 2 compartments. It's ownership passed from Pullman to the Chicago & Eastern Illinois in 1948. The car is pictured in set-out service at Orlando, Florida, in the mid-1950s. Note C&EI's distinctive small car-name lettering. *W. B. Cox, Krambles–Peterson Archive*

touring the West. By the late 1920s, the majority of the 24 private cars available for lease on the Pullman roster were each configured much like a railroad office car with sleeping, dining, and lounge facilities as well as an open platform. Pullman's 1924 private-car catalog did include one composite (baggage club) car, a parlor car, a few regular sleepers, and a tourist sleeper for those desiring to assemble a train.

The Pullman private car fleet numbered 34 in 1910, 24 in 1930, and 17 in 1940. The fleet was down to just 2 by 1944. The opulent way of life that the Pullman private car symbolized was largely a thing of the past by the end of World War II.

Changes to Pullman's standard car fleet came primarily in response to downturns in business as well as changes in customer preferences. The section, Pullman's primary accommodation, had always been a compromise in design. On the one hand, the design was very economical for Pullman. A section car carried one-third more passengers than a room car and

Knickerbocker was a 12-section,1-drawing-room car. The car wore silver paint when it was assigned to the Southern in 1941, then was repainted Pullman green in 1944. Sold to Southern in 1948, in 1949 the car received this elaborate shadow-lined paint scheme meant to mimic the stainless steel fluting of lightweight passenger cars delivered to the Southern. *J. Michael Gruber collection*

weighed 7,000 pounds less, but lack of privacy was inherent in its design. Two passengers (likely strangers) were forced to sit staring at each other all day and were separated from the aisle only by a curtain while sleeping. Likewise, the upper berth was impossibly claustrophobic. The coffin-like upper berth was not big enough to effectively undress or dress in and it also lacked a window. These drawbacks led to changing passenger tastes over time. Pullman and its customer railroads noticed the trend. By the 1930s, nearly 80 percent of passengers were choosing to travel in a lower berth. This left lots of empty space in section cars and often required the addition of extra sleeping cars to accommodate passenger demand for lower berths. This in turn added extra weight to the train, contributing to increased railroad operating costs. Pullman also incurred higher costs because every extra car it added required a porter to staff it.

These trends led Pullman to introduce more single-occupancy, all-room cars. In 1927, Pullman introduced Plan 3980, the *Night* series, with 14 single rooms. The single passenger now had the privacy he or she craved. The private single rooms in the cars offered 33 square feet of floor space and sold at a rate 25 percent more than a lower berth. The double bedroom made its debut in 1930.

Seeking to maximize the profit from its thousands of cars with low occupancy of upper berths, Pullman introduced a marketing campaign in 1930. The single-occupancy section, ironically nicknamed SOS, offered passengers the assurance that in exchange for an incremental fee they would not have to share their section with another passenger. It was a clever effort to turn an extra profit, since Pullman couldn't fill the upper berths anyway.

The experimental heavyweight duplex sleeper *Nocturne* is shown during the period it wore PRR red, between 1937 and 1951. The Pennsylvania Railroad owned the car and retired it in 1956. It was used in short-distance overnight service. *Bob's Photo*

Postwar Pullman-rebuild *Fir Hills* shows off its rarely photographed solid-gray paint scheme in a view taken at Atlantic City, New Jersey, in the early 1950s. It would be repainted two-tone gray by 1953. Note the solarium lounge two cars up painted for the *Orange Blossom Special. Photographer unknown, author collection*

The Pullman operating company was trying to squeeze more profit from its existing fleet with the SOS. Its car-building arm attempted to do the same thing through new design. In 1929, Albert Hutt patented the duplex rail-car design offering a split-level plan, which allowed more rooms per car and more revenue. Pullman tested the concept in 1931 when it rebuilt two cars, *Wanderer* and *Voyager*, from a pair of 16-section sleepers. In 1933, Pullman rebuilt two baggage cars into the *Eventide* and *Nocturne* cars. Unlike *Wanderer* and *Voyager*, which offered only a handful

of duplex rooms in an otherwise pedestrian layout, these new cars incorporated duplex rooms throughout. With only 16 duplex rooms, however, they would not provide enough accommodations to be economically viable. Nevertheless, a much-improved duplex sleeper concept would be at the center of Pullman's postwar car-building effort 13 years later.

Intent on improving its severely declining business and keeping its shop forces working during the Great Depression, Pullman embraced a completely new technology: air-conditioning. In 1929, Pullman

continued on page 90

Lake Caillou and other cars in the *Lake* series contained 10 sections, 1 drawing room, and 2 compartments. Union Pacific owned the car and leased it to Pullman. It was repainted from Pullman green to UP yellow on April 21, 1952. *Bob's Photo*

Lake Eleanor contained 10 sections, 1 drawing room, and 2 compartments. It was retained in Pullman ownership and assigned to the Pullman pool. It received its Pullman two-tone gray paint in December 1953. *J. Michael Gruber collection*

Clover Hollow was a Pullman betterment car with 8 sections and 5 double bedrooms. Rebuilt in 1935, it was stream-styled in October 1938 for assignment to the Baltimore & Ohio's *Capitol Limited*. Sold to the B&O in December 1948, it received its final paint scheme, shown here in January 1954 serving on the *Washington Express*. *J. Michael Gruber collection*

Glen Rae, a 6-compartment, 3-drawing-room car in the Pullman pool, was built in 1926 and repainted from green to two-tone gray in December 1954. *Harry Stegmaier collection*

Formerly named *White Bear Lake*, *Lariat Range* got its new name when it was modernized in 1940 for the *Texas Zephyr*. The car was painted solid silver in 1940, given shadow lines in 1949, and given the paint scheme seen here in 1954. Sold in 1948 to the Fort Worth & Denver City, a Burlington subsidiary, the car was withdrawn from Pullman lease in 1961. *Harry Stegmaier collection*

The updated postwar look of an open section in a Pullman heavyweight car is shown in this view from a Pullman training filmstrip. *Pullman photo, W. F. Howes Jr. collection*

continued from page 86

retrofit its first successfully air-conditioned car, *Mc-Nair*. By 1937, Pullman had air-conditioned approximately 3,300 of its own cars. At the same time, the company rebuilt hundreds of its cars with more useful floor plans. Often the floor plans included a mix of sections and Pullman's new, successful accommodation, the double bedroom.

Another change was the resurrection of Pullman dining service in the early 1930s, in response to the railroads' needs. The Depression had cut passenger train ridership by 40 percent nationally, and full diners weren't always necessary. This was especially true on roads with moderate ridership, such as the Wabash,

Erie, Chicago Great Western (CGW), Kansas City Southern, Nickel Plate (NKP), Chesapeake & Ohio, Rock Island, and Pere Marquette. Pullman stepped in to provide a less labor-intensive restaurant service in a series of combination cars that contained a mix of either sleeping sections and a restaurant, or parlor seats and a restaurant. It was a cost-effective way to replace railroad-operated full dining service, with its typical crew of four cooks, seven waiters, and a steward. Pullman service was provided by a crew less than half that size. Between 1932 and 1939, Pullman rebuilt approximately 79 cars to provide this restaurant service. At least two other cars were rebuilt

Pullman *Bryn Mawr College* contained 10 sections, 2 double bedrooms, and 1 compartment. It was painted for assignment to the Rio Grande Railroad's *Royal Gorge* in June 1955. *Krambles–Peterson Archive*

with buffet kitchens. These cars supplemented dozens of other existing cars built new in 1929 and 1930 that provided either restaurant or buffet service in addition to either sleeping or parlor facilities.

Pullman's delectable meals were served on daytime routes such as Pere Marquette trains from Chicago to Grand Rapids. Overnight travelers could also enjoy Pullman fare aboard trains such as Chicago Great Western's *Minnesotan* from Chicago to the Twin Cities; NKP's *Nickel Plate Limited* from Chicago to Cleveland; Texas & New Orleans' *Hustler* from New Orleans to Shreveport, Louisiana; or the Erie's *Erie Limited* between New York and Chicago. While

the service declined significantly after World War II, it was still possible to regularly enjoy Pullman meals on the PRR between Washington and New York, or on the *Bar Harbor Express* from Washington to Maine. The last survivors to offer some form of Pullman meal service into 1968, were New Haven's Pullman lounge on the *Federal* where a club breakfast was available, and Union Pacific's *Butte Special* where a converted section of a 6-6-4 *American* sleeper turned out modest meals.

Air-conditioning and new accommodations were nice, but the severe decline in railroad and Pullman passenger revenues spurred the companies to take

continued on page 95

Poplar Vista was rebuilt in June 1939. The *Poplar* series contained 6 sections and 6 double bedrooms. The car was sold to the Atlantic Coast Line in December 1948 and leased back to Pullman for operation. The car received this stunning paint scheme in July 1955. *J. Michael Gruber collection*

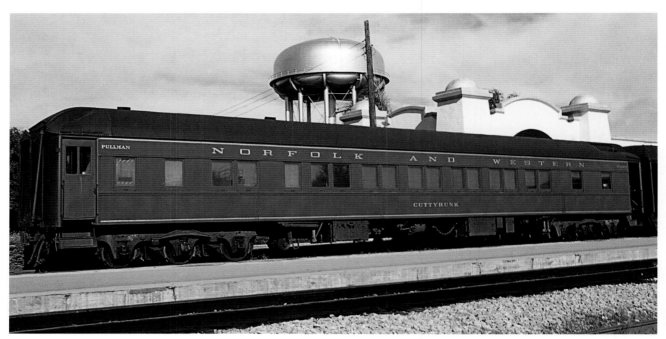

Norfolk & Western-owned *Cuttyhunk* was a 12-section, 1-drawing-room car. It is shown parked at Orlando, Florida, in June 1955. The car was painted its rich N&W Tuscan red with gold stripes and lettering in August 1953. The veteran car was withdrawn from Pullman service in 1962. *W. B. Cox, Krambles–Peterson Archive*

Nashville, Chattanooga & St. Louis purchased the Pullman *Rock Cabin* in 1948. The car had 8 sections, 1 drawing room, and 2 compartments. Painted in its owner's colors, it waits patiently for its next run in Orlando, Florida, in the mid-1950s. *W. B. Cox, Krambles–Peterson Archive*

Cars in Pullman's *Tower* series contained 8 sections, 1 drawing room, and 3 double bedrooms. *Castle Tower* was owned by Pullman but painted in Illinois Central colors in November 1956. *Bob's Photo*

ILLINOIS CENTRAL

MAIN LINE OF MID-AMERICA

Now—
Sleeping Car
Service
on the
Streamlined Diesel-Powered
City of Miami

SLEEPING CARS AND
RESERVED SEAT COACHES

continued from page 91

more radical steps. This translated into the development of streamlined, lightweight equipment in the mid-1930s. A transition to that trend was Pullman's *George M. Pullman* observation car. Constructed by Pullman in 1932, this car had many of the features of future streamlined cars. It was constructed of lightweight aluminum and weighed only 48 tons (a little more than half the weight of a heavyweight Pullman car). It also contained an enclosed, rounded solarium on the rear. Nonetheless, its window designs harkened back to Pullman's stodgy heavyweight cars. The *George M. Pullman* was indeed a one-of-a-kind transitional sleeping car, but it foretold the future. Just around the corner, Pullman would make history by building the first true American streamliner.

Dover Fort was one of nine cars rebuilt by Pullman in 1934 to contain 6 double bedrooms and a buffet lounge. The car was purchased by the New York Central in 1948 and leased to Pullman. It was painted the two-tone gray shown here in New Haven, Connecticut, in February 1958. *W. F. Howes Jr.*

Despite its heavyweight appearance, *Fir Range* was a late Pullman rebuild in 1950. It carried 6 sections, 4 roomettes, and 4 double bedrooms. It entered service in solid gray with silver lettering, then was painted two-tone gray in 1954 and received the Texas & Pacific blue shown here in 1959. The car was retired in 1964. *Harry Stegmaier collection*

Many heavyweight Pullman cars spent their last years in service south of the border. National Railways of Mexico sleeper *Amado Nervo* had previously been Pullman car *Orange Lake*. It was sold to NdeM in 1950 and withdrawn from Pullman lease, but re-entered Pullman lease in 1961. *W. F. Howes Jr.*

Sierra Madre was an 8-section, 5-double-bedroom sleeper owned by the Missouri Pacific and leased to Pullman. The car was painted in the exotic colors of the *Aztec Eagle*, a National Railways of Mexico train, in 1956. The car is shown in 1963, one year before being withdrawn from Pullman lease. *Harry Stegmaier collection*

PREWAR LIGHTWEIGHT CARS:

1932–1943

REFLECTING THE BROADER NORTH AMERICAN ECONOMY, the early 1930s was a period of great financial strain for The Pullman Company and its car manufacturing affiliate. Demand for new cars evaporated. Traffic and profits fell as business and vacation travelers retrenched in response to the ongoing Great Depression. Between 1932 and 1935, Pullman's sleeping car operations lost more than $3 million. Meanwhile, more and more of those individuals who were still traveling began to opt for the freedom of the automobile or the speed and prestige of the emerging commercial airlines. Pullman therefore sought to reduce the costs of passenger car construction, operation, and maintenance, while still recognizing the competitive need to provide appealing new equipment that operated on convenient, accelerated schedules.

In one of the top railroad photos of all time, the New York Central company photographer captured the 1938 *20th Century Limited* heading to Chicago under a setting sun in the beautiful Hudson Valley. *NYC photo, author collection*

The result was a fundamental change in the way that North American railroad passenger cars were designed and built, both in the materials used and how the cars looked. The influential trade publication *Railway Age*, in its June 3, 1933 issue, described the shift to new lightweight materials as marking "the third great evolution" in passenger car design, preceded by wood then heavy, fireproof steel.

Relatively new materials such as stainless steel, high-tensile Cor-Ten steel, and aluminum combined light weight with comparatively high strength, and by the early 1930s were readily available for commercial fabrication. To the railroads, this meant

that passenger train schedules could be accelerated and operating costs reduced. A five-car train of new lightweight cars, for example, could be conveyed more rapidly by a given locomotive, with corresponding fuel savings, than could a five-car train of older heavyweight cars. Similarly, a given locomotive could be expected to pull more lightweight cars, with correspondingly higher revenue per train, within that locomotive's tonnage rating. While the Edward G. Budd Manufacturing Company of Philadelphia worked to overcome the difficulties inherent in reliable stainless steel fabrication, Pullman's car-building arm embraced aluminum in 1933 as its

99

Mother and daughter enjoy the comforts of a prewar Pullman double bedroom in a still from a Pullman training filmstrip.
Pullman photo, W. F. Howes Jr. collection

favored structural material for passenger cars. The initial results of both builders' efforts were showcased in Chicago at the 1933–1934 Century of Progress Exposition, a lakefront world's fair conceived as a forward-looking salve for the Depression-inflicted economic scars of the United States.

Growing out of the European art deco design movement of the late 1920s, futuristic trends in art and architecture entered the North American mainstream as governments, led by President Franklin D. Roosevelt's New Deal administration, underwrote public works projects calculated to relieve unemployment while creating tangible glimpses of a Utopian post-Depression world. Whether in the air, on the sea, or on land, the adoption of streamlined forms for

transport vehicles in the early 1930s, regardless of the materials employed in their construction, coincided with the popularity of art deco design and its subsequent evolution.

In the air, the advent of streamlining was best exemplified by the Douglas DC-2 and DC-3 airliners. While not the first commercial monoplanes, their combination of rugged design, aluminum construction, and flowing lines would have considerable impact, positive and negative, on the North American passenger train. On the DC-3 and its airborne counterparts and successors, form followed function: Streamlining was a means of reducing aerodynamic drag and increasing speed and fuel efficiency. Similar benefits were sought by marine architects in designs
continued on page 105

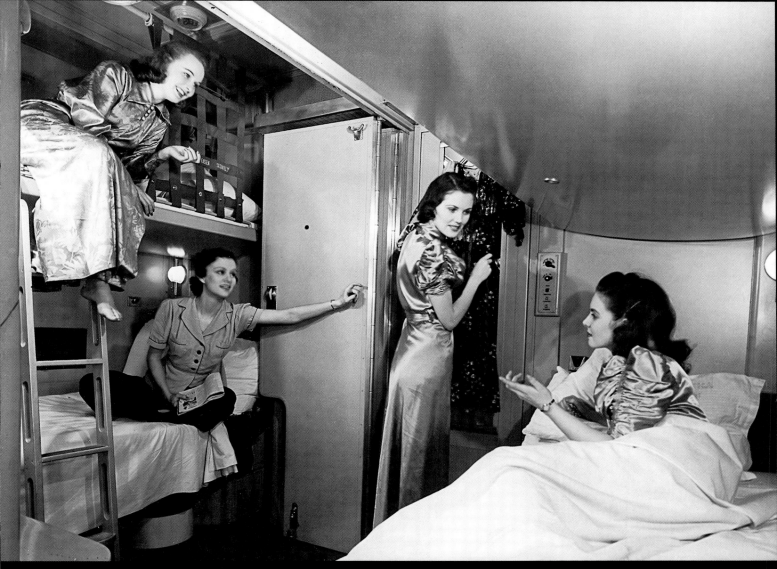

Bedrooms en suite provided travel fun in grand manner aboard the new Pullman double-bedroom cars. *PRR photo*

Pullman Sleeping Accommodations

FEW EXPERIENCES IN LIFE WERE AS COZY AND COMFORTING AS A RIDE IN A PULLMAN CAR. Traveling aboard a sleeping car with its plush interior, tucked into a well-made bed with its distinctive Pullman blanket while watching the landscape roll by outside your window was often an experience that remained a lifelong memory for passengers.

The size of your party and your wallet likely determined the type of Pullman accommodation in which you traveled. The company fielded a range of accommodations that slept one to three people. Some of Pullman's cars also offered the ability to arrange rooms en suite via the removal of a portable wall between rooms. Hence, two side-by-side double bedrooms might be arranged as an oversized room sleeping four passengers.

The following summarizes Pullman's most common accommodations at a time when the company's offerings were at their most varied in the period after World War II.

Section (One or Two Persons)

The section had two facing seats that could be folded down to form a lower berth; an upper berth folded down from above. Partitions or permanent walls separated sections from each other. At night, heavy curtains, each labeled with the section number, offered privacy from the aisle. The section was the least expensive and most common Pullman accommodation for the individual traveler. As Pullman passenger tastes changed over time the section became less popular, but even into the mid-1950s Pullman was building lightweight cars with sections.

Roomette (One Person)

Pullman introduced the roomette in 1937. It was the successor to the section and became the most popular single-person accommodation of the lightweight era. A marvel of efficiency, it featured a seat with a berth behind it that folded down from the wall, a picture window, small closet, a luggage rack, fold-down sink, and toilet. A wall with a sliding pocket door gave complete privacy. Up to 22 roomettes (11 on each side of a center aisle) could fit in a car.

Duplex Roomette (One Person)

Another design refined in the lightweight era, the duplex roomette had all the features of the roomette but in a slightly smaller space. Rooms were on two levels with up to 12 rooms on each side of the corridor. Space was saved by the duplex design in which part of each room was either above or below an adjacent one.

Duplex Single Rooms (One Person)

Though based on the same principle of partially overlapping rooms as the duplex roomette, the duplex single room was more spacious. The room was wider and located on only one side of the car. Equipped similarly to roomettes, duplex single rooms had wider sofa-sized seats, with backs that folded down to make berths that were crosswise to the car.

Double Bedroom, Type A (One or Two Persons)

Originally introduced in 1930, the double bedroom became one of Pullman's most popular accommodations postwar. A folding wall enabled two adjacent rooms—which each slept two — to effectively become one large room, making it ideal for parties of up to four people. Early types of double bedrooms such as this featured a toilet that folded into a cabinet under a sink. The design's major shortcoming was the lack of privacy afforded those using the toilet in a two-person room.

Double Bedroom, Type B
(One or Two Persons)
A major advance over the type A double bedroom (and similar type C), the type B featured a small room or annex for the sink and toilet. Instead of the sofas provided in the bedroom of types A and C, the type B bedroom seated its passengers on two armchairs. These were folded and stored under the lower bed at night.

Double Bedroom, Type D
(One or Two Persons)
The type D double bedroom came in two variations: the beds were either lengthwise or crosswise to the car. The lengthwise version had a roomette-like seat and an armchair for one, while the crosswise version had a sofa for two. Both contained an annex for a sink and toilet. The folding wall between rooms had a door that enabled passage between the rooms even when the partition was closed.

Compartment (One or Two Persons)
This enclosed accommodation for a party of two dates from the wooden-car era when it was called a "stateroom." A sink and toilet were standard in the room. Initially, the seat/berth arrangement resembled a section; later a sofa replaced two facing seats, resulting in a crosswise or lengthwise bed configuration. Compartments were larger than double bedrooms, and common in cars built until the end of the lightweight era.

Drawing Room
(One, Two, or Three Persons)
Also dating from the nineteenth century, the drawing room was for decades the standard Pullman accommodation for travelers who desired more deluxe accommodations than a section. Thousands of Pullman cars offered at least one drawing room. Features included three berths and enclosed sink and toilet facilities. Through the heavyweight era, the berths were lengthwise with two berths against the window and one lengthwise berth along the corridor wall. Lightweight-era drawing rooms had a sofa and lengthwise and crosswise berths.

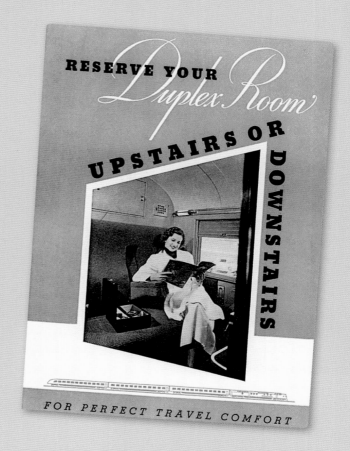

Silver Dollar, a 1936 product of Pullman, contained 12 open sections and was articulated (connected by a shared set of wheels) with observation car *Ogallala*. The two-car set brought up the rear of Union Pacific's *City of Denver* from 1936 to 1953. *Harry Stegmaier collection*

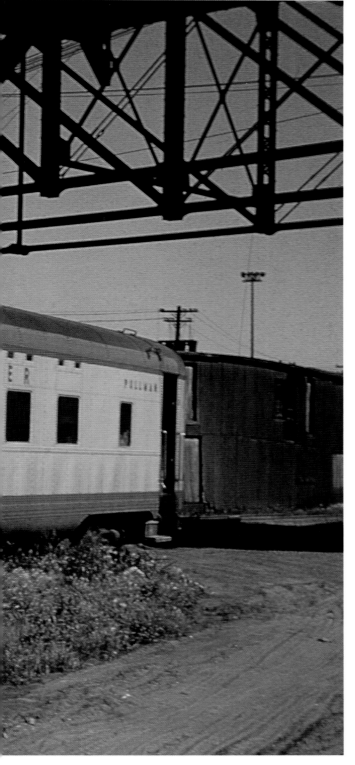

continued from page 100

of ships such as the French Line's *Normandie*, of 1932, where both hull and superstructure configurations were carefully calculated to speed the vessel on its highly competitive transatlantic crossings, while at the same time promoting an élan calculated to appeal to first-class and tourist passengers alike.

For the railroads, as it turned out, streamlining was more an exercise in public relations than in fuel efficiency. Studies showed that wind against a moving train, with the exception of a direct headwind or tailwind, resulted in increased resistance of wheel flanges against the downwind rail that negated the aerodynamic benefits of streamlining. The real benefits of this "new era in car construction," as *Railway Age* lauded it, were in the use of lightweight materials as a means of reducing operating costs while maintaining or improving safety standards, and in the publicity value of the streamlined trains' modernistic appearance and accommodations.

PULLMAN'S NEW ERA

Pullman launched its new era by displaying a pair of passenger cars at the 1933–1934 Century of Progress Exposition that were unlike anything the railroad industry had ever seen. At a glance, their shining bare-metal finish, flush windows, and tapered form presented a likeness more aligned with the new Douglas airliners than with the dark green Pullmans that fairgoers were used to seeing and riding.

Of the two aluminum-bodied cars—a coach and a sleeper, both built with round-ended observation lounges—the sleeping car claimed center stage at the exposition, thanks in no small measure to it being named for company patriarch George M. Pullman. The weight savings achieved through the use of aluminum was significant. The 84-foot-long sleeper tipped the scales at 96,980 pounds versus 180,000 pounds for a typical conventional Pullman car. Although Pullman chief engineer Peter Parke acknowledged that the initial designs of the two aluminum cars entailed extra effort, the ease of aluminum fabrication—in

Finished in natural stainless steel, *Muskingum River* brings up the rear of the *Arizona Limited* as it traverses the train's namesake state. The all-Pullman winter seasonal train between Chicago and Phoenix lasted only two seasons before being cut short by World War II. Ahead of *Muskingum River* are two Pullman *Imperial*-series sleepers, two Pullman *Cascade*-series sleepers, and a *Rock Island* diner and baggage-dormitory. *SP photo*

particular, the use of cost-effective extruded shapes—and inherent weight savings effectively signaled the end of the heavyweight passenger car era. With the exception of wheels, springs, axles, brake shoes, and friction-susceptible parts, the *George M. Pullman* was built entirely of riveted aluminum; even the car's insulation, in the form of crumpled foil, employed the metal. The remarkable weight reduction meant that six-wheel trucks, de rigeur for heavyweight Pullmans, could be replaced by lighter four-wheel designs on the two Century of Progress cars. Rare was the passenger car built after these two lightweight pioneers that required six-wheel trucks.

Like its coach-observation companion, *George M. Pullman*'s car-body exterior was unpainted, left instead in its natural polished aluminum finish and sealed with clear lacquer. Overseeing *George M. Pullman*'s interior and exterior decoration, consulting architect Samuel A. Marx accented the car's exterior with raised striping and lettering in gilded brass. Marx also specified natural aluminum for much of the car's interior surfaces. The overwhelming modernity was tempered somewhat by carpeting and upholstery that featured a classical Grecian wreath pattern, and by ash-and-ebony wood doors leading to the sleeping accommodations (3 double bedrooms, 1 compartment, and 1 drawing room). Behind the

sleeping area, a small buffet served a pair of four-seat dinette tables. The rear of the car was occupied by an 18-seat observation lounge.

PULLMAN LIGHTWEIGHTS TAKE TO THE TRACKS

The first lightweight Pullman sleeping cars built specifically for revenue service (as opposed to the conceptual *George M. Pullman*) were part of Union Pacific's six-unit articulated *City of Portland* train set. Built by Pullman-Standard in 1934, the train comprised a diesel-electric power car (M-10001), a baggage-mail car, three Pullman sleepers, and a coach-buffet car. By the time it entered revenue service in June 1935 following a barnstorming tour and mechanical improvements, a diner-lounge had been added to the train. Two of the *City of Portland*'s Pullman sleepers were 8-section, 1-compartment, 1-bedroom cars (*Overland Trail* and *Oregon Trail*). The third (*Abraham Lincoln*) offered 10 sections, 1 compartment, and 1 bedroom. *Overland Trail* had actually been the first lightweight articulated Pullman sleeper, built in February 1934 and exhibited as part of Union Pacific's pioneer streamlined M-10000 consist, although it never operated in revenue service in that train. Section accommodations in these cars were of a radical new semi-closed design, incorporating sliding aluminum partitions to replace the heavy curtains that

Imperial Highlands, a New York Central 4-4-2, wears the third livery of five it carried during its career. The prewar car is shown in model form as it appeared in 1946. *Model by W. F. Stauss, Keith Fink photo*

Garden of the Gods, built by Pullman for Rock Island's *Rocky Mountain Rocket* in 1939, contained 8 sections, 2 compartments, and 2 double bedrooms. The car is at Chicago's LaSalle Street Station in September 1949. *Bob's Photo*

Hidden Valley contained a popular prewar floor plan with 6 sections, 6 roomettes, and 4 double bedrooms. Once decorated in two-tone gray, the car is shown in the last paint scheme it received in 1956, solid gray with a silver roof. The car is shown on Santa Fe's train *The Grand Canyon* in July 1964. W. F. Howes Jr.

were all that separated made-down sleeping areas from the corridor in a traditional Pullman. Small curtains remained to provide a private dressing area jutting into the corridor space for every lower- and upper-berth occupant. Two "Tall Men's" sections in each car featured beds that were 6 inches longer than the Pullman standard of 72¾ inches. As originally built, all sections in the three cars incorporated folding washbasins and illuminated shaving mirrors in upper and lower berths (built into the corridor partitions). By the time the expanded train entered service as the *City of Portland*, the upper-berth basins and mirrors had been eliminated, as had folding armrests in the section seat backs.

In April 1935, Pullman announced that it was developing a two-unit articulated sleeping car to tour the United States in demonstration service in order "to enable railroad men to study streamline equipment in regular service" on the rear of conventional overnight trains. The lead car was intended to be a duplex design, containing 15 single bedrooms in an 8-upstairs, 7-downstairs configuration. This duplex arrangement was a streamlined, lightweight continuation of experiments embodied in Pullman's heavyweight *Voyager* and *Wanderer* cars of 1932, and *Nocturne* and *Eventide* of 1933. Transverse beds in these rooms converted to sofas for daytime occupancy like a regular Pullman bedroom. The design of the proposed trailing unit combined 4 double bedrooms with a buffet area and a round-ended observation lounge. Although similar in this respect to the *George M. Pullman*, renderings of the 1935 articulated duo depicted an advanced degree of streamlining, including teardrop-shaped shrouds over truck side frames and a full-width diaphragm cover between the two units. When the cars were completed in summer 1936, their names, *Advance* and *Progress*, were particularly appropriate, given the

course the duo charted for future lightweight car design and construction methods.

While aluminum was employed for much of the interior components, *Advance* and *Progress* were each framed and clad in low-alloy, high-tensile Cor-Ten steel. This would be the norm for subsequent Pullman-Standard passenger cars, although the riveted construction of *Advance* and *Progress* was replaced by welding. Exteriors were painted gunmetal gray with black and gold striping. Underbody equipment was concealed behind inward-curving metal skirts that hinged upward for maintenance access. When completed, *Advance* contained 14 duplex single rooms and 2 double bedrooms, a slight variation from the

1935 proposal. *Progress* emerged as a 3-bedroom, 1-compartment sleeper with a buffet and round-ended observation-lounge area. Generously sized, round-cornered thermal-pane windows were an improvement over *George M. Pullman*'s transitional glazing and, like the new cars' Cor-Ten girder-plate construction, would become the standard for most subsequent Pullman designs.

For the time being, though, UP remained an adherent of aluminum-bodied passenger cars, and additional articulated Pullmans entered UP service in 1936. Sharing the distinctive tubular cross-section and low profile of the *City of Portland* cars, the 1936 *City of Los Angeles* included 11-section Pullman cars (*Santa*

Anita, *Cinema*, and *Boulder Canyon*), 7-bedroom, 2-compartment car (*Mormon Trail*), and 11-section Pullman cars (*Hawaii*, *Honolulu*, and *Oahu*). In addition, 7-2 sleeping cars (*Lanai*) were built for Union Pacific's 1936 *City of San Francisco*. For a pair of 12-car *City of Denver* semi-articulated train sets, UP and Pullman abandoned the low-profile, tubular cross-section of their previous lightweight trains in favor of a taller, more conventional arrangement offering more interior cubic footage. For the 1936 *City of Denver*, Pullman-Standard built 12-section, 1-compartment, 1-drawing-room sleepers (*Cache la Poudre*, *Silver Dollar*, *Big Piney*, and *St. Vrains*); 8-section, 1-compartment, 2-bedroom cars (*Squaw Bonnet* and *Snowy Range*);

and 5-bedroom, 1-compartment observation-lounge cars (*Ogallala* and *Colores*). Similar in concept to *Advance* and *Progress*, two 12-1-1 Pullmans operated as articulated twin-unit cars in each of these *City of Denver* consists, as did the articulated 8-1-2 sleeper and sleeper lounge-observation car.

Even as articulated train designs flourished in the mid-1930s, railroads and equipment designers were aware of the concept's shortcomings as applied to passenger trains. It was a weight-saving compromise that reduced the number of trucks needed to support a train, but such semipermanent coupling of cars limited flexibility in car assignment. Inordinate effort, expense, and inconvenience were required to alter the consist of an articulated train in response to traffic or maintenance requirements. Accordingly, the vast majority of lightweight Pullman cars built before and after World War II did not employ articulation, and could therefore be assigned virtually anywhere services were needed.

As the new UP trains made headlines throughout the West, *Advance* and *Progress* commenced their demonstration careers in August 1936 with a one-week stint on New York Central, followed by a week on rival Pennsylvania Railroad. Even during these brief initial visits, the future of Pullman travel as embodied in *Advance* and *Progress* made a far-reaching impression on both railroads.

LIGHTWEIGHT-CAR REFINEMENT

The year 1936 ended with another significant development when the 8-section, 2-compartment, 2-double-bedroom car *Forward* was delivered to The Pullman Company by its Pullman-Standard car-building arm. Employing Cor-Ten steel in its mostly welded frame and side-truss framework (the latter a weight-reducing change from previous steel girder-plate side construction), *Forward*'s sides were sheathed in corrugated stainless steel panels evoking the hallmark exterior styling of up-and-coming rival

The *American Milemaster* was built to Pullman Plan 4082 in April 1939. Exhibited at the 1939 New York World's Fair, the car was named in a nationwide contest. Along with a similar car, *Muskingum River*, *American Milemaster* contained a floor plan with 1 drawing room, 1 compartment, 2 double bedrooms, a buffet, and an observation lounge. The car led an interesting life, seeing regular assignment to the *Arizona Limited*, *City of San Francisco*, and the Southern Pacific streamliner *Lark* before being rebuilt as a General Motors test car. It is still on the rails today. *W. F. Stauss collection*

car builder Budd. In *Forward*'s case, perhaps to minimize the inevitable comparisons, the stainless steel sides were painted in the same polychromatic gunmetal finish Pullman had used on *Advance* and *Progress*. Even though it employed steel and not aluminum in its exterior construction, *Forward* was still roughly 40 percent lighter than a comparable heavyweight Pullman car. Although subsequent lightweight Pullman construction would favor smooth, welded Cor-Ten side sheathing rather than corrugated stainless steel, *Forward*'s overall size, format, and mechanical layout presaged the widespread onset of Pullman's lightweight era. *Forward*'s first foray into revenue-service evaluation was on the Santa Fe, where the car operated as part of that road's premier *Super Chief* between Chicago and Los Angeles until mid-January 1937. After that it was sent on a wider tour.

In a 1939 address to the Society of Automotive Engineers, Pullman's chief engineer, Peter Parke, summarized the four approaches to lightweight passenger-car construction adopted by North American car builders over the preceding six years. Parke said that riveted, girder-type side construction using aluminum produced the lightest cars, but was the most expensive method and required particular care in determining a car design's limits of deflection under load, as aluminum was only about 30 percent as elastic as steel. Truss-frame construction employing stainless steel throughout produced strong, light cars but required the use of Budd's proprietary Shotweld process to overcome the difficulty of fabricating the corrosion-proof metal. In *Forward* and cars Pullman-Standard subsequently built for Santa Fe and Rock Island, the company opted to combine a bridge-like truss frame of low-alloy, rust-resistant, high-tensile Cor-Ten steel—a material readily welded—with a cosmetic covering of clip-on stainless steel panels. Similar to Budd's design, these thin, non-structural panels were corrugated, or fluted, for rigidity because flat panels made of such flimsy material tended to buckle and ripple. According to Parke, this construction method yielded a car that weighed roughly the same as a car of comparable all-stainless steel design but presented practical difficulties in locating window openings that did not conflict with the many angled

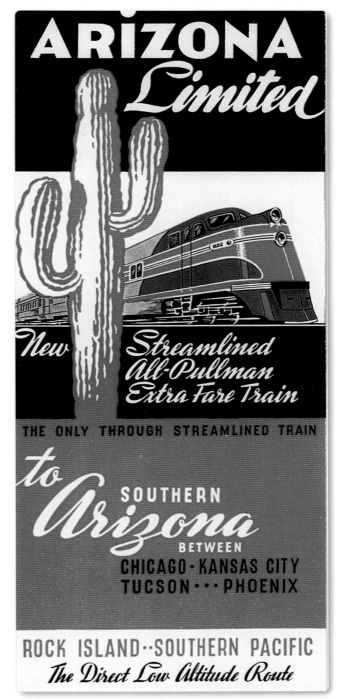

This colorful advertisement from 1940, the first season of the *Arizona Limited,* used a trademark cactus to entice Midwesterners to sunnier climes. The brochure also contained photos and floor plans of the cars. *Rock Island photo*

truss-frame members. Unappreciated at the time, too, was how years of electrolytic interaction between stainless steel and the underlying Cor-Ten frame would cause difficult-to-detect and often irreversible corrosion damage beneath the cars' stainless-steel exteriors. The fourth approach employed Cor-Ten steel throughout in welded-girder side construction to produce a smooth-sided car with a painted exterior. This last type of side construction allowed designers complete freedom in the placement of window and door openings, and was the method used in 1937 to build Pullman's experimental *Roomette I*.

Pullman touted its newest and most exciting accommodation in this *Roomette* advertisement. *Author collection*

The innovative roomette debuted in Pullman's car *Roomette I*. Tested on numerous trains, it heralded a major change in Pullman accommodations and inspired both the Pennsylvania Railroad and New York Central to implement all-room trains. *Pullman photo P43925, courtesy Bob's Photo*

This next experimental Pullman sleeping car was noteworthy more for its interior configuration than for its smoothly welded exterior. Pullman had long sought a cost- and space-effective replacement for its open section as more and more travelers expressed a preference for affordable private room accommodations. With this motivation, compounded by growing competitive pressure from the automobile and airliner, Pullman developed the roomette, a compact, self-contained room for one person that incorporated a sofa seat, a narrow foldaway bed, and complete toilet and foldaway washstand facilities—all within the same floor plan footprint as an open section. The trick, of course, was to fit as many roomettes into a car as possible, either exclusively or in conjunction with other accommodations, without sacrificing potential revenue. *Roomette I* offered 18 of the new spaces, 9 on either side of a straight-as-an-arrow central corridor. Sliding lockable metal doors gave access to each roomette, and a heavy curtain could be drawn across the door opening to maintain privacy when travelers opted to lower or raise their own bed. The porter with his berth key no longer had to be summoned for the task, although many passengers still opted for assistance. When the roomette bed was lowered, though, the seat disappeared and the toilet was inaccessible. Although the contortions imposed by an upper or lower berth were effectively a thing of the past, roomette occupants still needed a measure of agility. After roomettes were introduced on a large scale on NYC, PRR, and Santa Fe trains in 1938, their popularity resulted in fewer open sections in subsequent lightweight Pullman cars. All-section lightweight sleepers were exceedingly uncommon. Cars that incorporated 4 or 6 open sections with an assortment of private room accommodations were far more typical.

LIGHTWEIGHT SLEEPING CARS

The lightweight sleeping car, along with other car types, was prominent in 1938 with the re-equipping of three dominant railroads' premier passenger train fleets. In February, Santa Fe placed the first of 45 new lightweight Pullman-Standard sleepers in service on an expanded *Super Chief* operation and

continued on page 120

Sporting one of the virtually unpronounceable southwest Indian names Santa Fe was fond of applying to its early streamlined cars, *Hotauta*, a 1938 Pullman-Standard product, offered 14 sections on the *Chief*. The car is pictured at Belen, New Mexico, in June 1948. *Bob's Photo*

Announcing
THE NEW
Streamlined 20TH
CENTURY LIMITED
. . . . . Starting June 15, 1938
16 HOURS between NEW YORK and CHICAGO
The First All–Room Train in America

NEW YORK CENTRAL
THE WATER LEVEL ROUTE . . . . YOU CAN SLEEP

Billed as the world's greatest train, the New York Central's *20th Century Limited* lived up to its lofty billing. Behind a J-3a Hudson locomotive styled by the great industrial designer Henry Dreyfuss, the 1938 edition of the *Century* is pictured curving north along the road's Water Level Route en route to Chicago. *NYC photo, author collection*

The modern interior of Santa Fe's 14-section lightweight sleepers was highlighted in this 1938 color brochure. *Santa Fe photo*

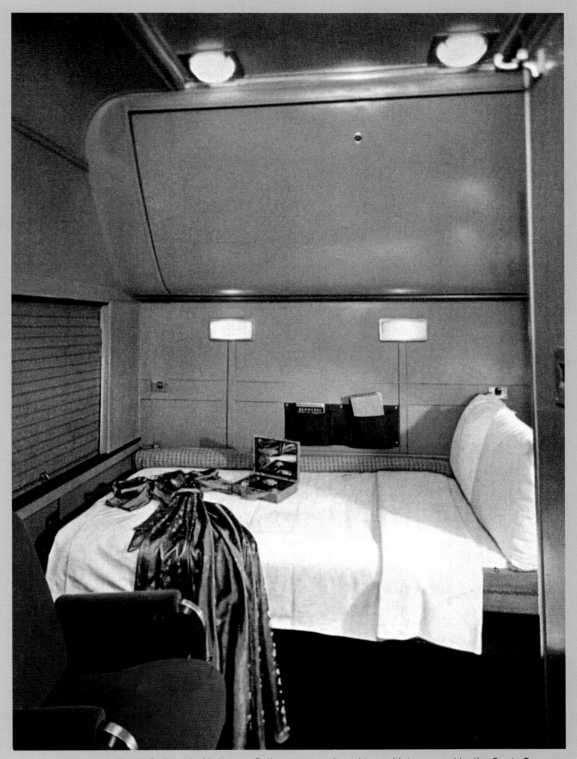

The drawing rooms in Pullman's *Mohave,* a Pullman car assigned to and later owned by the Santa Fe, were spacious and inviting. Stars of the silver screen were regular occupants of these cars. *Santa Fe photo*

Mohave was 1 of 12 sleeping cars with 4 double bedrooms, 4 compartments, and 2 drawing rooms that Pullman delivered for assignment to the Santa Fe's first streamlined version of its all-Pullman *Chief* between Chicago and Los Angeles. *Harry Stegmaier collection*

continued from page 115

other schedules. The new Pullman sleepers, based on *Forward*'s architecture and sheathed in unpainted stainless steel fluting, were configured as fourteen 8-section, 2-bedroom, 2-compartment cars; six 14-section cars; seven 17-roomette, 1-section cars; twelve 4-bedroom, 4-compartment, 2-drawing-room cars; and six 4-drawing-room, 1-bedroom, observation-lounge cars. On these all-roomette cars delivered to NYC, the mid-car section was not sold as revenue space. Rather, it was a place for passengers to wait in comfort while the porter attended to their roomette.

For Pullman and Pullman-Standard, the Santa Fe order delivered in 1938 represented much more than its first stainless steel-sheathed cars built for regular service. A car-building battle was brewing, and both *Forward*'s stainless steel cladding and the subsequent Santa Fe cars served as warning shots fired at upstart Budd by the Pullman interests. As Pullman saw things, it was entitled to be both sole builder and sole operator of railroad sleeping cars in the United States. When Santa Fe acquired two 8-section, 1-drawing-room, 2-compartment sleepers

(*Isleta* and *Laguna*), two 6-bedroom, 2-drawing-room, 2-compartment cars (*Oraibi* and *Taos*), and a 2-drawing room, 3-compartment, 1-bedroom, observation-lounge car (*Navajo*) from Budd in 1937, Pullman did not take the development lightly. Faithful Budd customer Burlington Route had triggered the confrontation when it purchased sleepers from the Philadelphia builder in 1936 for the re-equipped *Denver Zephyr*. Pullman reacted negatively. For example, it maligned the safety of Budd's sleepers and threatened to refuse staffing of sleepers that were not built by Pullman-Standard. Pullman's heavy-handed response to these perceived transgressions by Burlington and Santa Fe would have far-reaching repercussions for Pullman, Pullman-Standard, and the industry at large. Within a decade, as the result of a federal antitrust action filed in 1940, Pullman's long-held monopoly was broken. Retaining its then-lucrative car-building operation, Pullman opted to sell its sleeping car fleet to the railroads postwar. The railroads, in most instances, then contracted with a reconstituted Pullman Company for the cars' continuing operation.

STREAMLINED LIGHTWEIGHTS GO MAINSTREAM

Despite the emergence of competitive sleeping car builders, Pullman had much to celebrate. On June 15, 1938, NYC and PRR simultaneously unveiled the streamlined, lightweight re-equipping of their premier passenger trains, highlighted by an impressive assortment of new sleeping cars. For its *20th Century Limited*, NYC acquired 56 new Pullman sleepers. For a re-equipping of the *Broadway Limited* and other members of its *Blue Ribbon* fleet, PRR took delivery of 84 new Pullman through mid-1938, with some variation in floor plan. During development and construction, Pullman was at pains to cater to two of its most important railroad partners while at the same time keeping these railroads' deep-rooted competitive desires in check and resisting, wherever possible, their desire for costly and complicated customization of car interiors. As bitter rivals in the lucrative New York City–Chicago market, neither NYC nor PRR could be seen to have an advantage over the other in this high-profile fleet renewal.

continued on page 124

Pullman introduced cars with 13 double bedrooms, such as *Westchester County*, on the *20th Century Limited* and the *Broadway Limited* in 1938. The accommodation proved to be one of Pullman's most popular over the ensuing three decades. *Pullman photo*

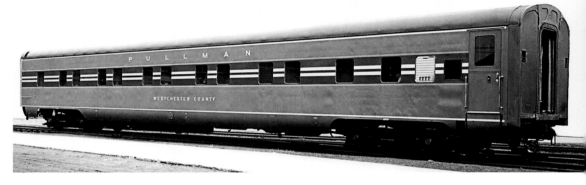

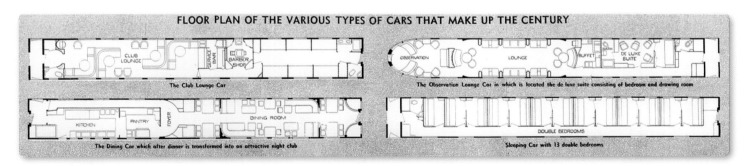

FLOOR PLAN OF THE VARIOUS TYPES OF CARS THAT MAKE UP THE CENTURY

The Club Lounge Car

The Dining Car which after dinner is transformed into an attractive night club

The Observation Lounge Car in which is located the de luxe suite consisting of bedroom and drawing room

Sleeping Car with 13 double bedrooms

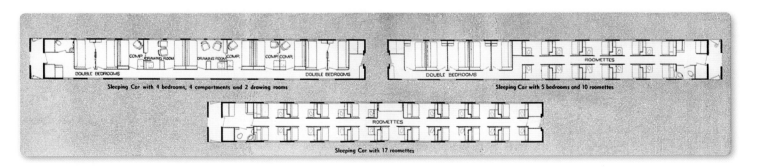

Sleeping Car with 4 bedrooms, 4 compartments and 2 drawing rooms

Sleeping Car with 5 bedrooms and 10 roomettes

Sleeping Car with 17 roomettes

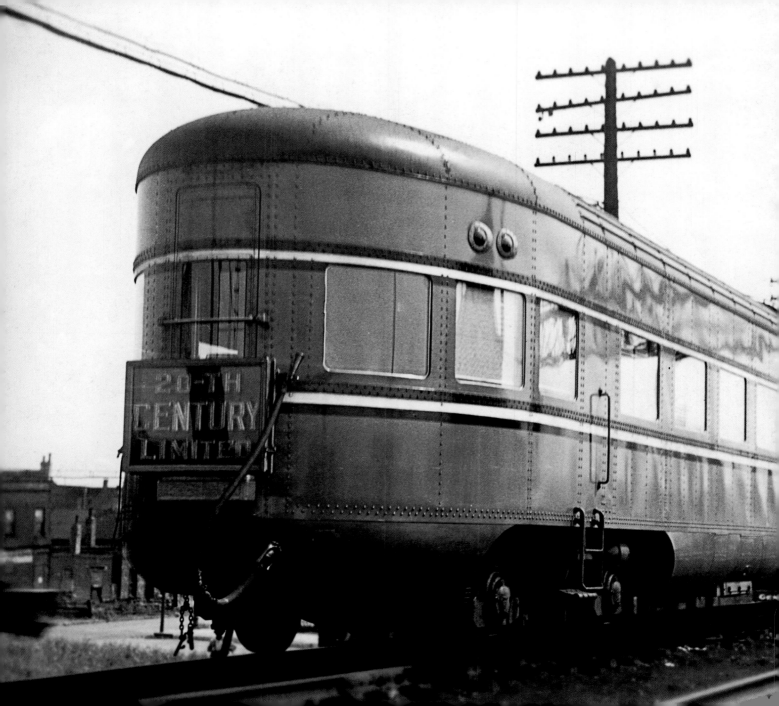

How would you like to travel--

UPSTAIRS OR DOWNSTAIRS?

Here is the "upstairs" room.

HERE's privacy with a touch of novelty! An ingenious "upstairs and downstairs" arrangement. When you travel in "Duplex" style it is like renting upstairs or downstairs living quarters. "Duplex" Single Rooms are arranged on two levels, and afford an added thrill in Pullman comfort. The Duplex Single Room is available on certain Eastern and Western trains. It's smart to travel in a "Duplex" room.

Stairs leading to "upstairs" rooms

AND what real travel comfort! At night your sofa becomes a sleep-inviting bed. Oh yes, Duplex occupants adjust weather conditions to their taste with individual control of the air-conditioning apparatus. They have individual toilet facilities and lighting control. The upper rooms have the locker above the sofa for luggage. In the lower room, luggage space is under the sofa and in an overnight rack.

And here is the "downstairs" room.

THERE are really a lot of conveniences. A table that folds against the wall. Ceiling and reading lights afford effective illumination. In some of the "downstairs" Duplex rooms, sliding panels make it possible to transform them into spacious suites. Some of the upper rooms have communicating doors. Large mirrors, folding washstands and cabinets with toilet accessories are part of the accommodation.

Pullman's experimental observation car *Progress* and its articulated mate *Advance* bring up the rear of the pre-streamlined *20th Century Limited* in 1937. *Photographer unknown*

continued from page 121

The all-room Pullman cars built for NYC and PRR—with not a single revenue open section among them—featured the smooth-sided architecture employed on the demonstrator *Roomette I.* The cars' floor plans offered a wide range of sleeping accommodations: 18-roomette (*City* series, PRR); 17-roomette, 1-section (*City* series, NYC); 4-bedroom, 4-compartment, 2-drawing-room (*Imperial* series); 13-bedroom (*County* series); 10-roomette, 5-bedroom (*Cascade* series); 12-duplex single room, 5-bedroom (*Brook* series, PRR); 2-bedroom, barber, secretary, bar-lounge (*Harbor* series, PRR); 3-bedroom, 1-drawing-room, bar-lounge (*Colonial* series, PRR); 1-master-room, 1-bedroom, buffet lounge-observation (*Island* series, NYC); 2-master-room, 1-bedroom, buffet lounge-observation (*View* series, PRR); and 2-drawing room, 1-compartment, 1-bedroom, buffet lounge–observation (*Narrows* series, PRR). The PRR car exteriors were painted in a predominantly Tuscan red scheme devised by Raymond Loewy's studio, while NYC cars were clad in a conservative two-tone gray designed by Henry Dreyfuss. So successful were the 1938 re-equippings that both railroads ordered additional cars for delivery in 1939 and 1940. NYC augmented its lightweight fleet with 82 more sleeping cars during this period, while PRR added 56 Pullman cars to its 1938 *Fleet of Modernism* by the end of 1940. At that time, a total of 388 lightweight sleeping cars were operating under Pullman Company auspices.

continued on page 127

Streamlined K4s Pacific-type locomotive 3768, styled by Raymond Loewy, earned the nickname "The Torpedo" from Pennsylvania Railroad crews. Here it leads the streamlined *Broadway Limited* eastbound out of Chicago on its inaugural run as a streamliner on June 15, 1938. *W. A. Ranke, author collection*

Pennsylvania Railroad's *Spirit of St. Louis* pauses at Altoona, Pennsylvania, on its nocturnal journey to its namesake city.
A. M. Rung, author collection

Raymond Loewy's *Fleet of Modernism* color scheme for the Pennsylvania Railroad is worn by the streamlined *Liberty Limited* at Englewood, Illinois, in 1939. *Dan Peterson, Harry Stegmaier collection*

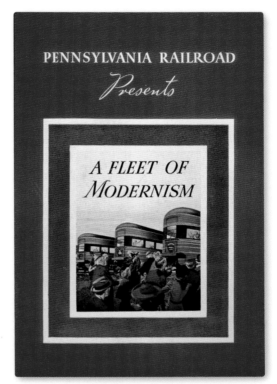

PRR introduced travelers to its *Fleet of Modernism* streamliners with this colorful brochure. *PRR photo*

continued from page 124

By the end of 1941, new or re-equipped trains incorporating lightweight, streamlined Pullman sleeping cars were also operating on the Rock Island (*Rocky Mountain Rocket* and *Choctaw Rocket*), Baltimore & Ohio (*Capitol Limited* and *Ambassador*), Denver & Rio Grande Western (the short-lived, self-propelled but underpowered Budd *Prospector*), and Southern Pacific (*Lark*).

Continuing its quest to boost revenue and reduce operating costs by squeezing the maximum number of desirable room accommodations into a single sleeping car, Pullman unveiled the demonstrator car *Duplex Roomette I* in 1942. The car's 24 roomettes were slightly smaller than those the public had come to know, and its 12-up, 12-down arrangement made use of every scrap of space inside the car. The war effectively made this car an orphan; a dozen stainless-steel-sheathed examples delivered by Pullman-Standard in 1948 as Santa Fe's *Indian* series and 20 examples built by Canadian Car & Foundry in 1949 for Canadian National were the only other 24-duplex roomette cars.

Southern Pacific's all-Pullman streamliner *Lark* made up for its late-1941 entrance into the streamliner field with its stylish good looks. Here a classic GS-4 steam locomotive dressed in *Daylight* orange and red leads the southbound *Lark*'s gray consist into Glendale, California. *Bill Olson, courtesy Tom Gildersleeve slide productions*

Interestingly, Budd went in the opposite direction when it introduced the chambrette in 1939. The chambrette was a single-occupancy room, slightly larger than a roomette, with a folding chair in place of the roomette's fixed sofa seat and aligned so the lowered bed was transverse to the car's centerline (roomette beds were always positioned lengthwise). Two cars built in 1939 to augment the Burlington Route's *Denver Zephyr* (*Silver Slipper* and *Silver Moon*), and the trailing cars of Rio Grande's two twin-unit *Prospector* trains of 1941 (*David Moffatt* and *Heber C. Kimball*) were the only lightweight cars constructed with chambrettes.

The last new blocks of Pullman cars built before U.S. involvement in World War II curtailed production were assigned to Erie Railroad, Illinois Central, Missouri Pacific, and Southern Pacific in 1942, and to Baltimore & Ohio in 1943. A quartet

of *American*-series 6-6-4 sleepers went to the Erie. Illinois Central received a total of 20 revenue sleepers for the Chicago–New Orleans *Panama Limited*, while Missouri Pacific employed a quartet of 6-6-4 Pullman-Standard sleepers in the otherwise all-Budd consists of its St. Louis–Denver/Colorado Springs *Colorado Eagles*. Southern Pacific and Rock Island were assigned thirteen 6-6-4 and fifteen 4-4-2 Pullman-Standard sleepers in 1942 for assignment to the *Golden State* and shared in a group of 60 *American*-series 6-6-4 Pullman cars and 18 *Imperial*-series 4-4-2 cars delivered in 1942 for joint service with Overland Route partners Union Pacific and Chicago & North Western. A trio of 10-5 Pullman-Standard cars assigned to Baltimore & Ohio in September and October 1943 (*Cascade Drive*, *Cascade Sound*, and *Cascade Music*) were the final new sleepers delivered until production resumed after the war.

Top: The classic round-end observation car of Southern Pacific's *Lark* pauses at Glendale, California, on its nocturnal journey between Los Angeles and the Bay Area. *Bill Olson, courtesy Tom Gildersleeve slide productions*

Left: *Cascade Sound*, a Baltimore & Ohio–assigned 10-roomette, 5-double-bedroom car was one of three 10-5 sleepers assigned to B&O in September and October 1943, at the height of World War II. The car is shown postwar painted in Missouri Pacific colors for service on that road. *Harry Stegmaier collection*

For a full measure of travel pleasure....
Ride Union Pacific
Streamliners

DAILY BETWEEN CHICAGO
AND LOS ANGELES · PORTLAND
SAN FRANCISCO · DENVER

Coach or Pullman

UNION PACIFIC RAILROAD

The 4-4-2 became the streamlined-era equivalent of Pullman's heavyweight-era 6-compartment, 3-drawing-room cars. The 4-4-2 cars operated on a number of the top trains in the country, offering Pullman's most expensive accommodations. The cars also worked in the Pullman pool. Union Pacific's *Imperial Bird*, delivered in 1942, is shown here at Green River, Wyoming, in 1958 wearing Illinois Central colors for its temporary assignment to that road's *City of Miami* train. *Jack Pfeifer, author collection*

POSTWAR CARS:

1945–1968

AS A RESULT OF A 1944 FEDERAL ANTITRUST DECISION AGAINST THE PULLMAN COMPANY, Pullman was ordered to divest itself of either its manufacturing or its operating arm. Pullman chose to keep the lucrative manufacturing business. The operating company, which provided sleeping car, parlor car, and some dining service to the railroads was put up for sale and eventually purchased by a group of 57 (later 59) railroads.

The Santa Fe *Super Chief* (background) meets train No. 201, the Denver–La Junta, Colorado, connecting train at La Junta on April 28, 1971. One of the greatest names in railroading, the *Super Chief* had been an all-Pullman train for much of its career. This view, taken 2½ years after Pullman's demise and just days before Santa Fe exited the passenger train business on May 1, shows the sleeping car portion of the train. *Bob Schmidt*

Perhaps the most noticeable change from this business shift was that the new first-class sleeping and parlor cars built postwar were now owned by the railroads, and were leased to and operated by Pullman under contract. Pullman previously owned almost all the cars it operated, but as a result of the 1944 court decision it was ordered to sell much of its equipment. In December 1945, Pullman sold 601 lightweight sleeping cars and 256 (mostly heavyweight) parlor cars to the railroads at a cost of over $35 million. The railroads then leased the cars to Pullman to operate. Pullman also issued "car notes," essentially dividends to its owner railroads, which reduced the railroads' investment in Pullman stock from

$40 million to $27 million. Subsequently, the railroads took ownership of an additional 2,444 heavyweight Pullman cars. Pullman retained ownership of 2,875 heavyweight cars and 6 lightweight cars. These cars formed the backbone of Pullman's pool, a flexible source of capacity that could, for example, be used to cover seasonal fluctuations in demand or unexpected troop movements.

Another noticeable change that resulted from the breakup of Pullman was that new cars built for Pullman assignment had to be purchased directly from the car builders. The railroads were in a frightening hurry to buy those cars. The travel impacts of World War II, when rail travel demand quadrupled, had

continued on page 136

133

Above: American Car and Foundry delivered nine sleeping cars to the Lackawanna Railroad in 1949. The cars contained 10 roomettes and 6 double bedrooms, and were finished in the railroad's stunning maroon and gray color scheme. *ACF Industries*

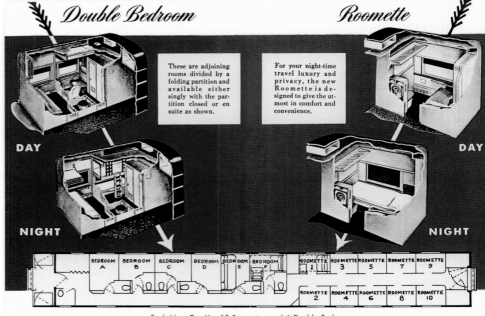

Double Bedroom

These are adjoining rooms divided by a folding partition and available either singly with the partition closed or en suite as shown.

DAY

NIGHT

Roomette

For your night-time travel luxury and privacy, the new Roomette is designed to give the utmost in comfort and convenience.

DAY

NIGHT

Each New Car Has 10 Roomettes and 6 Double Bedrooms

Luxury ~ Convenience ~ Privacy

The connecting double bedroom is a luxury accommodation suitable for two or four persons. Both rooms have full-sized upper and lower beds, and each room is equipped with private enclosed toilet and washstand, individual heat control and air conditioning. Circulating cool water, wardrobe lockers, full-length mirrors, electric razor outlet, ample luggage space, shoe lockers, arm rests and convenient lighting facilities complete the bedroom designed for family or business travel.

The new Roomette is for the passenger who wants all the advantages of a private room at low cost. It is designed for single occupancy and utilizes every inch of floor space to advantage. A comfortable bed folds down from the wall and is pre-made. Each Roomette has its own toilet and washstand, full-length mirror and clothes locker. The Roomette is fully air conditioned, with separate heat controls for individual regulation. There is ample luggage space, cool drinking water, an electric razor outlet, and convenient lighting.

These new cars have been given names of Indian origin identified with the territory served by the Lackawanna.

Right: Lackawanna released this now-rare brochure to tout its new streamlined sleeping cars. It contained a floor plan. *Author collection*

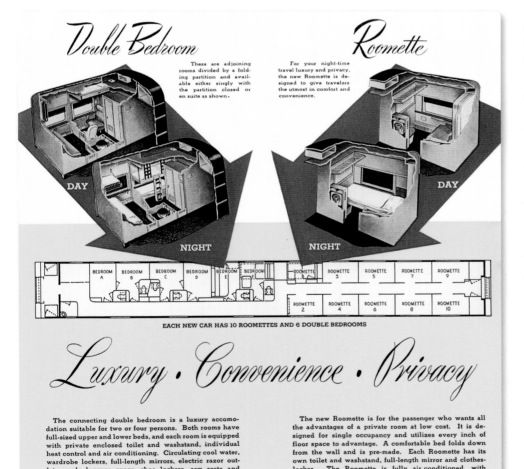

Double Bedroom

These are adjoining rooms divided by a folding partition and available either singly with the partition closed or en suite as shown.

Roomette

For your night-time travel luxury and privacy, the new Roomette is designed to give travelers the utmost in comfort and convenience.

DAY

NIGHT

DAY

NIGHT

| BEDROOM A | BEDROOM B | BEDROOM C | BEDROOM D | BEDROOM E | BEDROOM | ROOMETTE 1 | ROOMETTE 3 | ROOMETTE 5 | ROOMETTE 7 | ROOMETTE 9 |
| ROOMETTE 2 | ROOMETTE 4 | ROOMETTE 6 | ROOMETTE 8 | ROOMETTE 10 |

EACH NEW CAR HAS 10 ROOMETTES AND 6 DOUBLE BEDROOMS

Luxury · Convenience · Privacy

The connecting double bedroom is a luxury accommodation suitable for two or four persons. Both rooms have full-sized upper and lower beds, and each room is equipped with private enclosed toilet and washstand, individual heat control and air conditioning. Circulating cool water, wardrobe lockers, full-length mirrors, electric razor outlet, ample luggage space, shoe lockers, arm rests and convenient lighting facilities complete the bedroom designed for your traveling comfort.

The new Roomette is for the passenger who wants all the advantages of a private room at low cost. It is designed for single occupancy and utilizes every inch of floor space to advantage. A comfortable bed folds down from the wall and is pre-made. Each Roomette has its own toilet and washstand, full-length mirror and clotheslocker. The Roomette is fully air conditioned, with separate heat controls for individual regulation. There is ample luggage space, cool drinking water, an electric razor outlet, and convenient lighting.

Above: Built to Pullman Plan 4140, Norfolk & Western's *Buchanan County*, along with two other mates, arrived from Pullman-Standard in 1949. The cars often held down interline assignments from New York to Virginia points via an interchange with the Pennsylvania Railroad. *Buchanan County* is pictured in Norfolk & Western's modern station at Roanoke, Virginia. *Harry Stegmaier collection*

Left: This Norfolk & Western brochure advertised the road's new sleeping cars and contained a floor plan of the *Buchanan County* and its two sister cars. *Author collection*

continued from page 133

worn out older equipment and prematurely aged even newer prewar streamlined equipment. Competition was increasing as well. Between 1946 and 1954, America spent $20 billion on highway construction. In 1956, the country enacted federal legislation to create a 40,000-mile Interstate Highway System. However, even prior to the advent of the Interstate, Americans bought 37 million new autos postwar.

The airline industry also was a growing threat. By 1950, Pullman and the domestic airlines each handled about 16 million passengers annually. Pullman's business dropped to 13 million passengers by 1953, the same year airlines carried 26 million passengers. By 1958, competition was incredibly stiff, overwhelming Pullman. Still, in the decade after World War II, American railroads re-equipped their

continued on page 145

Pullman-Standard delivered eight sleeping cars to the Kansas City Southern in 1948. Dressed in the railroad's distinctive livery of dark green with yellow and red stripes, the *William Edenborn* and mates offered 14 roomettes and 4 double bedrooms. *Harry Stegmaier collection*

Catalpa Falls was one of 11 cars delivered to the Pennsylvania Railroad in 1949 with 6 double bedrooms and a buffet lounge. The car was built to Pullman plan 4131. Mid-train lounges like this could be found on numerous members of the Pennsylvania Railroad's *Blue Ribbon* fleet. *Harry Stegmaier collection*

Arguably the most exotic postwar Pullman cars were the seven dome sleeper-observation cars built by the Budd Company for the *California Zephyr*. With 3 double bedrooms, a drawing room, a dome that sat 24, an under-dome lounge, and a round-end solarium lounge, they were the ultimate cars on America's ultimate streamliner. *George Krambles, Krambles–Peterson Archive*

This cutaway from a 1949 brochure on the *California Zephyr* graphically illustrates the upstairs-downstairs arrangement of the car and its many features. *CB&Q, D&RGW and WP photo*

Santa Fe took delivery of fifteen 4-4-2 sleepers from ACF in 1950. They supplemented 16 other similar cars delivered by Pullman-Standard in 1948. Named in the *Regal* series, they operated in Santa Fe's top trains, such as the *Super Chief* and the *Chief*. *American Car and Foundry Archives, John W. Barriger III National Railroad Library, University of Missouri–St. Louis*

Santa Fe received one additional *Vista*-series observation car from ACF in 1950 to supplement four similar cars delivered by Pullman-Standard in 1947. The cars contained 4 drawing rooms and 1 double bedroom. They operated on the *Super Chief*. *American Car and Foundry Archives, John W. Barriger III National Railroad Library, University of Missouri–St. Louis*

Exemplifying the complexity of the Pullman system, the northbound Gulf, Mobile & Ohio *Abraham Lincoln*, a day train from St. Louis to Chicago, carries three interline Pullman cars on the rear: a Fort Worth–Chicago sleeper and a Houston–Chicago sleeper in Missouri Pacific blue, as well as a Mobile–Chicago sleeper in GM&O red. The date is December 7, 1955. *R. V. Mehlenbeck, Krambles–Peterson Archive*

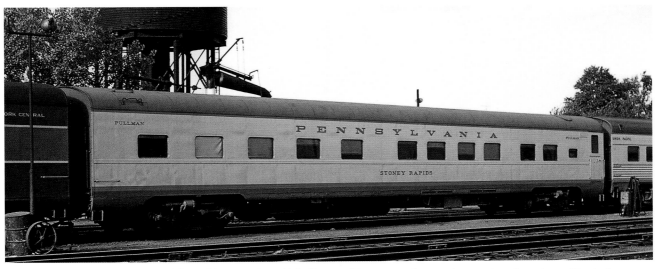

Pennsylvania Railroad, which participated in a number of interline services connecting western and southwestern cities to the eastern seaboard, rostered Pullman cars painted for connecting roads. At one point postwar, various PRR Pullman cars wore numerous paint schemes. The railroad's *Stoney Rapids* is pictured painted for through service in the Union Pacific's *City of Los Angeles* in the 1950s. *Lawson K. Hill, Chuck Blardone collection*

The Car Builders

FROM THE BEGINNING OF ITS CORPORATE LIFE PULLMAN LARGELY BUILT THE PASSENGER CARS IT OPERATED, but by the 1930s that had begun to change. In the headlong rush to modernize before World War II, some railroads found themselves ordering numerous passenger cars, including some sleeping cars, from other car builders, such as the Budd Company of Philadelphia (a relative newcomer to railroading). Budd built beautiful sleepers for both the first streamlined Santa Fe *Super Chief* and the Burlington Route's 1936 *Denver Zephyr*. Concerned about losing revenue, Pullman attempted to obstruct Budd's business by telling both Santa Fe and CB&Q that it would only operate a certain (small) number of sleeping cars built by Budd. Not surprisingly, Budd saw this as a threat to business and its protestations resulted in the government filing a federal antitrust suit against Pullman in 1940. In 1944, the courts ruled that Pullman either had to build cars or operate them. It couldn't do both. In 1947, the Pullman Operating Company was sold to a group of railroads, and Pullman Incorporated stayed in the more lucrative business of building cars.

The antitrust ruling changed the playing field for builders. With railroads now owning their own sleeping cars and leasing them to Pullman for operation, the railroads were free to order new sleeping cars from any builder they chose. This situation, coupled with the fact that railroads were desperate to re-equip their trains as soon as possible after World War II, resulted in a proliferation of orders for new Pullman cars to the three major car builders of the day: American Car and Foundry, Budd Company, and Pullman-Standard Car Manufacturing Company.

American Car and Foundry

American Car and Foundry (ACF) was formed in 1899 through the consolidation of 13 car-building firms. ACF produced passenger and freight cars as well as

Wabash Railroad received a total of 10 cars with 12 roomettes and 4 double bedrooms from American Car and Foundry. Six of the cars were used in local line service and were named in the *Blue* series. Another four Wabash 12-4 cars were named in the *Western* series and were originally used in interline service with Union Pacific on the *City of St. Louis*, between St. Louis and the West Coast. *American Car and Foundry Archives, John W. Barriger III National Railroad Library, University of Missouri–St. Louis*

Eagle Oak was one of 11 cars with 10 roomettes and 6 double bedrooms built by American Car and Foundry for the Pennsylvania Railroad and painted in Missouri Pacific colors for interline service on that railroad's *Texas Eagle. ACF Industries*

rolling stock for streetcar, interurban, and rapid transit systems. One of ACF's two principal plants was at St. Charles, Missouri, 20 miles west of St. Louis. This shop began building passenger cars in 1866. The company's other major facility was at Berwick, Pennsylvania. Originally the plant of the Jackson and Woodin Company, Berwick came under ACF ownership in 1899.

Prior to World War II, ACF constructed streamlined sleeping car accommodations as part of the Gulf, Mobile & Northern's pioneering *Rebel* streamliner,

although the accommodations weren't operated by Pullman. Between 1946 and 1956, ACF produced more than 900 conventional streamlined passenger cars. Among them were dozens of sleeping cars and a handful of parlor cars for a number of railroads, such as the Pennsylvania, Union Pacific, Wabash, and Santa Fe. American Car and Foundry was renamed ACF Industries in 1954. ACF quit the passenger business in 1961, by which time it had delivered 155 more passenger cars.

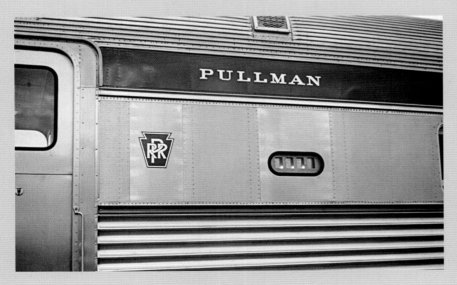

Details on the *Miles Standish*, a Budd-built parlor car for the Pennsylvania Railroad, included elegant small PRR keystone logos on the pier panel. Pennsylvania Railroad's parlor cars were operated by Pullman until 1956, at which time the railroad began operating the cars itself. *Budd Company photo*

Budd Company

The Budd Company was founded in 1916 as a successor to the Edward G. Budd Manufacturing Company, which had been organized to build steel automobile bodies. Budd's first significant railroad effort, in 1931, was a series of experimental cars with rubber-tired wheels built in partnership with the French firm Michelin. These were the first stainless steel railcars in America, setting a trend that lasts to this day. In 1934, Budd made history with the delivery of CB&Q's three-car stainless steel *Zephyr*, the first diesel-powered passenger train. After constructing the original *Zephyr*, Budd built a series of other great trains, including the CB&Q *Denver Zephyr* (1936) and the Santa Fe *Super Chief* (1937), both of which included the first examples of Budd-built sleeping cars that were operated by Pullman.

After World War II, Budd shifted production from its Hunting Park plant in central Philadelphia to its suburban Red Lion facility, where it turned out some of the most beautiful trains and individual cars of the era.

Included were hundreds of sleeping cars for railroads such as CB&Q, UP, and Santa Fe, to name a few.

Between 1946 and 1956, Budd delivered more than 1,200 passenger cars to a host of North American railroads. However, Budd's inventiveness didn't stop there. In the 1950s the company built innovative double-decked hi-level intercity cars for the Santa Fe (the inspiration for today's Amtrak Superliners). Budd also built the versatile and cost-effective Rail Diesel Cars (RDCs) of the 1950s. In the 1960s the company delivered the *Metroliners*, the train that made the New York–Washington route the only true high-speed passenger line in America and which led to today's Amtrak *Acela Express* trains. Budd also delivered hundreds of Amfleet cars that formed the backbone of the Amtrak fleet beginning in the mid-1970s. The Budd Company went through a variety of changes until, in April 1987, Budd ended all railcar production at its Red Lion plant in northeast Philadelphia. Eventually its rail design legacy ended up as part of the Bombardier Corporation.

The Budd Company produced hundreds of sleeping cars postwar, including entire train sets delivered for the Southern Pacific's re-equipped *Sunset Limited* in 1950. Among the groups were 25 mid-train sleepers with 10 roomettes and 6 double bedrooms. SP No. 9016 is pictured in the 1960s. Note the oversized nameplate with the train name on the car side. *Harry Stegmaier collection*

Pullman-Standard Car Manufacturing Company

George M. Pullman originally chartered Pullman's Palace Car Company in 1867. The company built passenger cars for decades at a variety of locations. As time passed, Pullman concentrated the construction of passenger cars at two principal locations. Most of its cars were created at its most famous location, the company's car works in Pullman, Illinois, which opened in 1881. Pullman also built cars at its Osgood Bradley plant in Worcester, Massachusetts. Osgood Bradley had been building cars for much of the 1800s and was assimilated into the Standard Steel Car Company in 1910.

In 1900, the Pullman Palace Car Company became simply The Pullman Company. The Pullman-Standard Car Manufacturing Company was created in 1934 as a subsidiary of Pullman Incorporated. Pullman-Standard was the product of Pullman's acquisition of the Standard Steel Car Company in 1930.

Pullman created the very first streamliners, Union Pacific's M-10000 in 1934 as well as a host of other streamlined cars until World War II. Following the war, Pullman-Standard built the influential *Train of Tomorrow* for General Motors, plus cars for nearly every major railroad. In addition to being the granddaddy of all postwar car builders, Pullman-Standard was the biggest, delivering more than 2,300 intercity passenger cars between 1946 and 1956, plus another 288 between 1956 and 1971. Hundreds of sleeping cars and parlor cars were included in the mix. Pullman-Standard also built Amtrak's first *Superliner* cars in the late 1970s.

With perhaps the longest road name in passenger railroading, Richmond Fredericksburg & Potomac was a key bridge line between Richmond and Washington, D.C. *Stratford County* was one of four RF&P cars in a group of 42 delivered by Pullman-Standard in 1949 for Atlantic Coast Line service from the northeast to Florida. *W. B. Cox, Krambles–Peterson Archive*

continued from page 136

trains at an amazing rate. Over 4,400 lightweight railroad passenger cars were constructed and the industry spent over $1.3 billion (in 1950s' dollars) on new equipment. These new cars were made of lightweight metals, streamlined in appearance, and finished in attractive colors or stainless steel. Among the 4,400 cars built postwar, the railroads purchased 1,603 modern, lightweight sleeping cars for lease to Pullman. They were well engineered and beautifully appointed. In what turned out to be a futile effort to assure prompt delivery and avoid long wait times, the railroads spread their orders for new Pullman cars among all three of the major car builders: American Car and Foundry, Budd, and Pullman-Standard.

The new Pullman cars came in a staggering variety of designs and floor plans. Pullman, which had always depended on standardization to keep its operating costs under control, complained to car-buying railroads about floor plans that added to costs and delayed the delivery process, confused ticket agents, and introduced diverse mechanical systems that at times created maintenance headaches. But despite some minor shortcomings, the new equipment invigorated a service suffering from a reputation of being old and outdated. While almost all room types introduced in postwar sleeping cars were based on types created immediately prewar or earlier, there were intelligent upgrades. For example, the Pullman lightweight bedroom received enclosed lavatory facilities, a necessary improvement in a room that seated two passengers.

The double bedroom would turn out to be one of the most successful Pullman accommodations in the fleet. A number of railroads ordered streamlined cars containing nothing but double bedrooms. Prewar streamlined cars containing 13 double bedrooms operated on roads such as the New York Central, the

continued on page 150

Union Pacific's all-Pullman version of the *City of Los Angeles* between Chicago and Los Angeles is shown on Wyoming's Sherman Hill sometime in the early 1960s. UP operated the popular streamliner in two sections—one coach, one all-Pullman—for many summers between 1956 and the mid-1960s. *Union Pacific Railroad Museum*

As part of its contribution to the pool of cars for the *Cascade* from Oakland to Portland, Northern Pacific purchased two sleeping cars to cover its share as it forwarded an Oakland–Seattle sleeper north of Portland. NP sleeper No. 364 is shown here, repainted from Southern Pacific two-tone gray into NP colors in the 1960s. *Harry Stegmaier collection*

Gulf, Mobile & Ohio received four sleeping cars from ACF with an unusual floor plan containing 8 roomettes, 1 compartment, 3 double bedrooms, and 4 sections. *American Car and Foundry Archives, John W. Barriger III National Railroad Library, University of Missouri–St. Louis*

...the preferred route
between Chicago and St. Louis

Gulf, Mobile & Ohio

- Union Station, Chicago, to Union Station, St. Louis . . . convenient downtown depots in other cities.
- Hostess Service on all day trains.
- Convenient departures, around the clock.
- High-speed double track and rock ballast.
- Diesel power for safe, smooth, swift speed. All trains.
- Automatic electric signals.
- Air-conditioned for year-'round comfort.

The G M & O is a *neighborly* railroad—a railroad where your first ride makes you a welcome guest, and your second ride a valued friend. For courteous service and complete dependability, seasoned travelers prefer the G M & O!

NOW...GM&O PRESENTS

Newest

IN SLEEPING CAR ACCOMMODATIONS

- Now in service, Chicago-St. Louis-Mobile, are the world's newest, most modern sleeping cars. They provide a variety of accommodations — with all the appointments needed to give you a smooth ride and sweet dreams.

Gulf, Mobile & Ohio leading the way betv

Gulf, Mobile & Ohio released this brochure that contained a floor plan for its unique sleeping cars. *GM&O photo*

Louisville & Nashville purchased three sleepers painted in Tuscan red for through service with the Pennsylvania Railroad. For several years, *Green River* held down a regular assignment between New York and Nashville, operating on the *Cincinnati Limited*. The car is pictured here in the consist of the *South Wind* operating between Chicago and Miami. *Harry Stegmaier collection*

THE

LUXURIOUS COMPARTMENT provides roomy privacy...and complete facilities for comfortable daytime or nighttime travel for two travelers.

SPACIOUS BEDROOMS also accommodate two people, affording restful surroundings and complete privacy day and night. For larger families...a double compartment or bedroom arrangement is available.

COMPACT ROOMETTES are for the passenger traveling alone. They're perfect for single occupancy ... with all the features of the larger rooms.

THRIFTY BERTHS provide traditional Pullman comfort . . . at somewhat less cost. Choose upper or lower, as you prefer.

...ween St. Louis and Chicago for over a century ...

The Pullman Fleet:
How Pullman Assigned Cars

AS A NATIONAL TRANSPORTATION COMPANY, THE PULLMAN SYSTEM WAS FAR FLUNG AND DIVERSE. Its cars visited remote corners of the United States from Key West, Florida, to Walla Walla, Washington, and seemingly everywhere in between. Some cars even went to parts of Mexico and Canada. Once committed, Pullman service had to be available for passengers to board on the advertised schedule despite weather or any of the other many challenges encountered in providing a transportation service. Often the company's cars arrived or originated in the consist of a train at a major station with complete services available and spare cars to cover any eventuality. But just as frequently a Pullman car would terminate at a local station with no services and little chance of replacement. With commitments like that, the system had to work like a well-oiled machine. It did because of Pullman's attention to detail. First and foremost, moving a fleet of nearly 100,000 rolling hotel rooms around the country every night required an elaborate system to keep track of the cars in which those rooms resided. It was all accomplished in the age before computers.

The assignment of Pullman cars to a particular railroad, route, and train was typically dictated by Pullman's contracting railroads. They would request specific floor plans of cars (each with a certain quantity and type of accommodations) to meet traffic demands. To track the cars and handle the accounting, Pullman managed its cars in "lines." Each Pullman car line linked two geographic endpoints on a railroad. The types of cars assigned to a line varied over time as did the endpoints. Pullman was constantly adjusting both its services and endpoints in response to changing customer needs.

Managing these lines was a complex undertaking. Some car assignments were extremely predictable. Lounge cars and observation cars assigned to the top trains usually enjoyed long-term assignments to those trains, as they had been ordered specifically for that service. However, most car assignments varied considerably. Sleeping cars came in groups built to the same floor plan and hence were often interchangeable. Sleeping cars on the Pennsylvania Railroad, for example, routinely changed formal assignments to different trains during the periodic reissue of the railroad's Pullman car assignment memo.

Controlling car assignments was the province of Pullman's superintendent of transportation. The superintendent managed the routine assignment of cars on both a large and small scale. His job included overseeing the gathering of hundreds of Pullman cars each fall coming out of service from summer traffic routes for assignment to railroads such as the Seaboard Air Line and Atlantic Coast Line (which experienced great demand for Pullman space to Florida every winter). The superintendent's job also involved the day-to-day minutiae of revising regular Pullman car assignments on dozens of railroads. Generally, Pullman issued two- to three-car assignment revision memos each year to the average railroad. These assignments were not written in stone, however, and in the words of one railroader, Pullman car assignments often deviated from the intended, seemingly before the ink had dried on the superintendent's memos. Bad-ordered cars required immediate mechanical attention and fell out of car line assignment (a regular occurrence), necessitating replacement cars added in their stead. Likewise, each regularly assigned Pullman car was due for routine heavy maintenance every 30 to 36 months. When the cars came out of line, they were replaced with the best available cars with a similar floor plan. For example, in the early 1950s, a Northern Pacific duplex roomette sleeping car held down a regular assignment on Milwaukee Road's overnight train *Pioneer Limited* for a time, with its two-tone green paint disrupting the *Limited*'s solid line of lovely orange and maroon cars.

It was a complex job, but the Pullman superintendent of transportation had help in the form of both his local staff and a series of managers below him at locations around the country. These Pullman district superintendents often handled short-term requests from railroads. Baltimore & Ohio, for example, kept a ready supply of extra heavyweight sleepers under lease to handle tour groups and military moves. When the railroad needed these cars or others from the Pullman pool, it usually contacted an on-line Pullman office whose job it was to gather and prepare the cars for travel over the road. Postwar, it was necessary for Pullman to request permission from the owning railroad to assign the railroad's surplus cars still in Pullman lease to cover needs on other lines. Most of the time, the railroad acquiesced—keeping its cars in actual assignment meant more revenue for the owning railroad.

Perhaps the greatest challenge in the car assignment arena came when an extremely late train made it impossible to field a regular train on the return leg. Then, the full resources of Pullman and the railroad would be brought to bear to ensure that passengers had an adequate train of replacement cars for their journey. Usually Pullman was up to the challenge, especially in later years, for as its traffic declined its available pool of surplus cars increased. Pullman, like the Post Office, never slept and rarely let inclement weather impact its mission. Indeed Pullman and the railroads generally came to the rescue when bad weather grounded planes by the dozens and passengers needed to get to their respective destinations.

Tracking the cars on a daily basis required the car desk clerks at Pullman's 86 districts and agencies to report the condition of arriving cars, so the company could ensure that a Pullman car would be available to return in working order. This was accomplished via telegraph, Teletype, or telephone. Due to the ex-

pense of using Western Union telegraph, Pullman developed an elaborate code system with hundreds of coded messages to reduce the number of words sent in each communication. For example, the word "garret," when used in a telegram, meant a 12-section, 1-drawing-room car. To report that a car was bad ordered and out of service because of bad wheels upon arrival, for example, the code word used was "barley." So the statement, "Barley *Chippewa Creek bad wheels*" meant "car *Chippewa Creek* cut off account bad wheels should be shopped for repairs. Please advise." In return, the telegraph from the local district might read, "Fern *Conewago Creek*, *Chippewa Creek*," which coded, "You may use *Conewago Creek* to relieve *Chippewa Creek* for shopping."

With Pullman operating a system of sleeping cars that were set out or picked up by through trains at various intermediate locations around the country, it was inevitable that the company had issues to manage at the end of the line. The destinations for set-out cars were diverse and often remote. At backwoods layover locations that lacked a Pullman organization such as Burlington, Vermont; Oil City, Pennsylvania; or any one of a hundred other far-off places, the set-out car would lay over by itself. The Pullman car's porter slept on the car and received a stipend for cleaning it when no other Pullman staff was available.

Sometimes when a car was bad ordered at a remote location there was no other option but to cancel the return revenue trip. Nevertheless, when Pullman cars arrived at a major destination, full services and an often sizable surplus fleet of replacement cars were available to address the problem. Even when problems occurred at small town locations near a larger hub, Pullman would make every effort to address the problem by sending in a replacement car from the big city when it could. It was all part of the complex game of managing a massive fleet of cars. It happened hundreds of times every day and the Pullman organization was supremely organized, trained, and equipped to get the job done.

continued from page 145

Pennsylvania Railroad, and the Southern Pacific. Postwar cars with the same accommodations contained fewer bedrooms. For example, NYC and SP received all-bedroom cars with 12 double bedrooms, while the Union Pacific, Seaboard Air Line, C&O, and Illinois Central ordered cars with 11. Seeing the growing popularity of the bedroom, some roads such as Santa Fe, PRR, Southern, and Atlantic Coast Line even rebuilt other types of cars into all-bedroom floor plans postwar.

Likewise, the fully enclosed roomette, sleeping one passenger and incorporating a seat, bed, sink, toilet, closet, and picture window, replaced the lower berth as the most desirable accommodation for the single traveler. Continuing the prewar trend,

the roomette, either by itself or combined with other types of sleeping accommodations, was incorporated into hundreds of new postwar Pullman cars. Between 1937 and 1950, 218 all-roomette cars were completed. Prewar cars typically contained 17 or 18 roomettes, while new postwar cars offered either 21 or 22. Postwar cars with this floor plan were originally delivered for service on NYC, PRR, SP, Rock Island, and ACL trains.

The most successful streamlined sleeping car floor plans contained a combination of roomettes and double bedrooms. Of these, the most common were cars containing 10 roomettes and 5 double bedrooms (10-5 floor plan) or 10 roomettes and 6 double bedrooms (10-6 floor plan). The layout had just the right ratio

Pullman out-shopped nine cars in December 1954 with 5 double bedrooms, 1 compartment, 4 roomettes, and 4 sections. The cars were built for the new *Dixieland* train operated jointly by the Chicago & Eastern Illinois; Louisville & Nashville; Nashville, Chattanooga & St. Louis; Atlantic Coast Line; and the Florida East Coast railroads. *Florida Flowers* was one of two cars built for C&EI. *Harry Stegmaier collection*

Loblolly Pine was one of 29 *Pine*-series sleepers out-shopped by Pullman-Standard in 1953. Four cars were owned by Chicago & Eastern Illinois, three by the Nashville, Chattanooga & St. Louis, and the remainder by the Louisville & Nashville. The cars contained Pullman type-S accommodations with a revised design in response to customer preferences. The *Pine*-series cars contained 6 type-S roomettes, 6 type-S sections, and 4 type-S bedrooms. *Harry Stegmaier collection*

New cars containing nothing but sections were rarities postwar. Union Pacific received 14 cars named in the *Alpine* series in 1954. Each contained 14 sections. The cars were used briefly on the *City of Portland* and the *Challenger*. They were rebuilt into leg-rest coaches in 1965. *Alpine Scene* is pictured in the 1950s. *Harry Stegmaier collection*

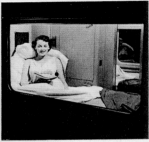

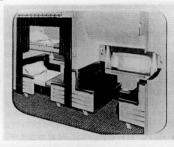
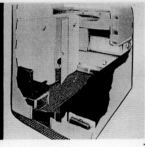

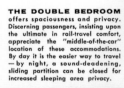
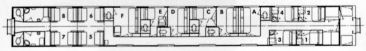

The brochure for the 1954 version of the *Dixieland* illustrated the interiors of the 5-1-4-4 sleepers and provided a floor plan. *C&EI photo*

of rooms to meet the needs of both single travelers and groups. Pullman produced 106 prewar 10-5 cars. A handful of 10-5 cars were created postwar, albeit with a different floor plan than the prewar version. Postwar, the three major car builders built a whopping 682 of the 10-6 floor plan, which had one more double bedroom than the 10-5. As a result, the 10-6 operated in every corner of the country and formed the backbone of many sleeping car fleets. The 14-4

with a mixture of 14 roomettes and 4 double bedrooms was a close cousin to the 10-6. These cars types operated on the New Haven, Missouri Pacific, Katy, Frisco, Southern Railway, and Kansas City Southern. Similarly, Union Pacific, Chicago & North Western, T&P, B&O, and Wabash all received cars with 12 roomettes and 4 double bedrooms.

Used only experimentally before World War II, the duplex roomette rose to popularity after the

Introduced experimentally prewar, the duplex roomette was used extensively by Pullman postwar. With 24 duplex roomettes, Santa Fe Pullman cars in the *Indian* series, such as *Indian Song*, boasted a floor plan with more duplex rooms than any other car. *Indian*-series cars were assigned to the railroad's *San Francisco Chief* and the *Texas Chief. Harry Stegmaier collection*

Boston & Maine sleeper *Hampton Beach* was renamed *Dartmouth College I* in 1961. Sister car *Old Orchard Beach* was renamed *Dartmouth College II* the same year. Both cars, and two others with the same floor plan on the Bangor & Aroostook, contained 6 sections, 6 roomettes, and 4 double bedrooms. *Harry Stegmaier collection*

war. It was incorporated into many new Pullman cars with varying floor plans. A western road, the Santa Fe, operated a series of cars containing only 24 duplex roomettes. Other roads such as C&NW, Baltimore & Ohio, Great Northern, Northern Pacific, Milwaukee Road, CB&Q, SP&S, and Rock Island offered cars with a mix of accommodations, including duplex roomettes.

While the number of new section cars built declined precipitously following World War II, the railroads continued to order cars with the accommodation, most frequently incorporating it in new floor plans with a mix of sections, bedrooms, and roomettes. Pullman's larger, higher-priced accommodations garnered the company more revenue, but the continued use of sections was largely to cater to government traffic. Prewar, 213 lightweight cars with 6 sections, 6 roomettes, and 4 double bedrooms had been built. Postwar, a significantly smaller number of cars with a mix of accommodations including sections continued to be delivered to a handful of railroads. These new cars went to UP, C&NW, ACL, SAL, Chicago & Eastern Illinois, Nashville Chattanooga & St. Louis, Louisville & Nashville, New

continued on page 158

Delivered to the Rio Grande Railroad in 1950 as 10-roomette, 6-double-bedroom sleepers, *Brigham Young* and three mates were rebuilt a year later with half their roomettes becoming open sections. The rare conversion in which the more popular roomettes were replaced by sections was motivated by federal travel restrictions, which would pay for government employees to travel only in a lower berth. *Krambles–Peterson Archive*

The Pullman sleeper-observation car continued to be produced in healthy numbers postwar. Among the most attractive of these cars were two built for service on the *Texas Special* between St. Louis and Texas points. The Katy's *Stephen F. Austin* is pictured on the rear of the *Texas Special* at Waco, Texas, in 1954. *Photographer unknown*

The interior of Seaboard Air Line's *Sun Lounge* is pictured in this 1958 view. *Jim Scribbins*

Starlight Dome was one of three dome sleepers acquired by Baltimore & Ohio from the Chesapeake & Ohio in 1951. The cars contained 5 roomettes, 1 single bedroom, and 3 drawing rooms. They were assigned to the *Capitol Limited* and the *Shenandoah*. *Harry Stegmaier collection*

continued from page 154

Haven, Boston & Maine, Bangor & Aroostook, and Florida East Coast. The D&RGW even rebuilt some postwar lightweight cars, replacing some of their modern roomettes with open sections.

Postwar cars containing nothing but sections operated briefly on three famous streamliners in the West. The new *California Zephyr*—introduced by D&RGW, Western Pacific, and Chicago, Burlington & Quincy in 1949—contained cars with 16 sections built by the Budd Company. UP introduced the ACF-built *Alpine* series of cars with 14 sections on its *City of Portland*, between Chicago and Portland,

Oregon; and on the *Challenger*, between Chicago and Los Angeles, in 1954. Both groups of cars were later rebuilt into coaches, as demand for open-section accommodations declined even more precipitously in the 1960s.

Nearly 175 cars containing 4 double bedrooms, 4 compartments, and 2 drawing rooms were built before and after World War II. They provided Pullman's most expensive, commonly assigned accommodations and could be found on the top trains in the country such as the Santa Fe's *Super Chief*, Pennsylvania Railroad's *Broadway Limited*, New York Central's

Dome sleepers were perhaps the rarest postwar Pullman car type. A total of 11 dome sleepers of this type were out-shopped for assignment to the *North Coast Limited* in 1954. Originally finished in Northern Pacific's two-tone green scheme, Spokane, Portland and Seattle's lone dome sleeper No. 306 received this rarely photographed, home-road scheme in the late 1960s. *Harry Stegmaier collection*

20th Century Limited, and many others. Postwar, UP and SAL ordered similar cars with 5 double bedrooms, 2 compartments, and 2 drawing rooms. Most commonly named in the *Imperial* series, the 4-4-2s were also often used in Pullman pool service. For this reason it was often possible to find Santa Fe or UP 4-4-2 cars running to Florida in the winter. Postwar, UP and SAL ordered similar cars with 5 double bedrooms, 2 compartments, and 2 drawing rooms.

Often traveling more than 15 hours on their journey, many Pullman passengers needed some distraction outside their rooms. Pullman cars that provided a mixture of sleeping rooms and first-class lounge space were also important members of the postwar fleet. These cars typically contained a mix of bedrooms and a buffet lounge where beverages and snacks were dispensed. Some of the lounge cars also offered light meals. Cars of this type were used mid-train and could be found postwar on roads such as the NH, NYC, PRR, ACL, SAL, UP, MP, and

Nickel Plate Road. The most exotic Pullman mid-train lounges were the Seaboard Air Line's three Sun Lounge cars delivered in 1956, equipped with 5 double bedrooms and a glass-enclosed lounge. The cars were assigned to the *Silver Meteor* streamliner (New York to Miami).

The postwar Pullman observation cars were more interesting cousins to the mid-train lounges. Assigned to the top trains in the country and some lesser-known ones as well, observation cars provided similar accommodations and services as the mid-train Pullman lounges. The postwar-built Pullman observation car contained a buffet and a mix of sleeper accommodations, and featured a completely enclosed solarium that offered a fine view of the railroad. These were considered the signature car of the streamliners to which they were assigned, and unlike other Pullman sleepers and lounges, which often rotated in their assignment, the observation cars were generally assigned long term to a specific train.

A Pullman conductor lifts a passenger's ticket in a Pullman double bedroom. The conductor holds a Pullman car diagram. *Pullman photo, W. F. Howes Jr. collection*

A white-jacketed Pullman lounge car attendant waits on a passenger in the lounge section of a postwar Pennsylvania Railroad *Falls*-series car. *Pullman photo, W. F. Howes Jr. collection*

Numerous 4-4-2 sleeping cars were delivered to various railroads postwar. *Imperial Loch* was one of 15 such cars delivered to the Pennsylvania Railroad for service on its top trains such as the *Broadway Limited, Pittsburgher,* and *Spirit of St. Louis. ACF Industries*

Top: The rounded interior of the rear lounge of Santa Fe's *Vista Club* is shown in this pre-delivery publicity photo. *American Car and Foundry Archives, John W. Barriger III National Railroad Library, University of Missouri–St. Louis*
Bottom: Looking toward the sleeping accommodations from the rear lounge of Santa Fe's *Vista Club. American Car and Foundry Archives, John W. Barriger III National Railroad Library, University of Missouri–St. Louis*

One of the most innovative Pullman cars of the postwar period was the Sun Lounge, which offered 5 double bedrooms and a buffet lounge. Operating in territory where clearances didn't allow a dome above roof level, the glass-enclosed roof of the car's lounge section simulated a dome. The three cars were assigned to Seaboard Air Line's *Silver Meteor* between New York and Miami. *M. Herson, Dave Ingles collection*

Trackside observers knew they could find *Mountain View* and *Tower View* bringing up the markers of the *Broadway Limited*; *Gulfport*, or *Memphis* on the rear of Illinois Central's *Panama Limited* from Chicago to New Orleans; a beautiful *River*-series car on Baltimore & Ohio's *National Limited*; and *Hickory Creek* or *Sandy Creek* on the rear of New York Central's legendary *20th Century Limited*.

Pullman operated even more exotic floor plans and car types. Among the most unusual were dome sleepers on the B&O; NP; Burlington (CB&Q); and Spokane, Portland & Seattle Railway; and dome sleeper observation cars on the CB&Q, D&RGW, and WP, which offered rooftop views for first-class patrons. A Pullman dome parlor service was also available on the Wabash Railroad. Cars with Pullman's most expensive accommodation, the postwar master

room, contained spacious quarters for two passengers (including their own shower, a luxury not available on almost any other accommodation at that time). This room type could only be found in two observation cars assigned to Pennsylvania Railroad's *Broadway Limited*, and in a series of four mid-train sleeper-lounges for Southern Railway's *Crescent Limited*.

Parlor cars that featured first-class daytime accommodations (usually plush, rotating chairs) never comprised more than about 3 percent of the total number of passenger cars operating nationwide. After the war, new lightweight parlor cars were largely confined to eastern roads such as PRR and the NH—except for a small number of cars built for a handful of midwestern and western roads, most of which provided their own parlor service. New Haven replaced most of its heavyweight parlor car fleet with dozens

The interior of the *Red Mountain's* buffet lounge was done in tones of brown and gray. Behind the bulkhead with the artwork was a buffet where the attendant dispensed beverages and snacks. *Both ACF Industries*

of streamlined lightweight cars in the late 1940s. The cars were used in many NH trains, including the road's top two trains, the *Merchants Limited* and *Yankee Clipper*, both operating between New York and Boston. Indeed, for a brief period after the war *Merchants* remained the last all-parlor car train in the nation. Coaches were added to it later. In 1952, the frugal PRR chose to replace parlors operating only on its top day trains, the *Congressionals* between Washington and New York and the *Senator* between Washington and Boston. Both NH and the PRR

contracted with Pullman to operate their parlor service until 1956. Along with the Wabash, they were the last three railroads to use Pullman for parlor service.

These new streamlined Pullman cars and many repainted heavyweight Pullman cars came in a rainbow of paint schemes and finishes. Reflecting the trend of the day, the railroads sought to distinguish their trains with bright new colors or shining stainless steel. The days of the ubiquitous, heavyweight Pullman green sleeping car were fading.

continued on page 170

Seaboard Air Line's *Red Mountain* was one of three Pullman sleeper lounges delivered by ACF to SAL. They contained 6 double bedrooms and a buffet lounge, and served most of their careers on the railroad's *Silver Star*. *ACF Industries*

Budd Slumbercoach cars for the Northern Pacific railroad were operated by Pullman. *Loch Rannoch*, shown here, started life as New York Central Sleepercoach No. 10801 in 1959. It was sold by Budd to Northern Pacific in 1964 at which time it received its name. *Harry Stegmaier collection*

A large number of sleeping cars with 6 sections, 6 roomettes, and 4 double bedrooms were delivered prewar. Postwar, a smaller number were produced, including 6 cars produced by ACF in 1950 for assignment to the Chicago & North Western/Union Pacific streamliners. *American Sunset*, delivered in that order, was repainted from UP yellow to C&NW colors in March 1956, a few months after C&NW ceased joint operation with UP. *Harry Stegmaier collection*

In 1952, Budd constructed a number of parlor cars for the Pennsylvania Railroad's *Congressional* (Washington, D.C.–New York) and *Senator* (Washington, D.C.–Boston) trains. *Miles Standish* featured 29 comfortable parlor chairs and an enclosed drawing room. *Budd Company photo*

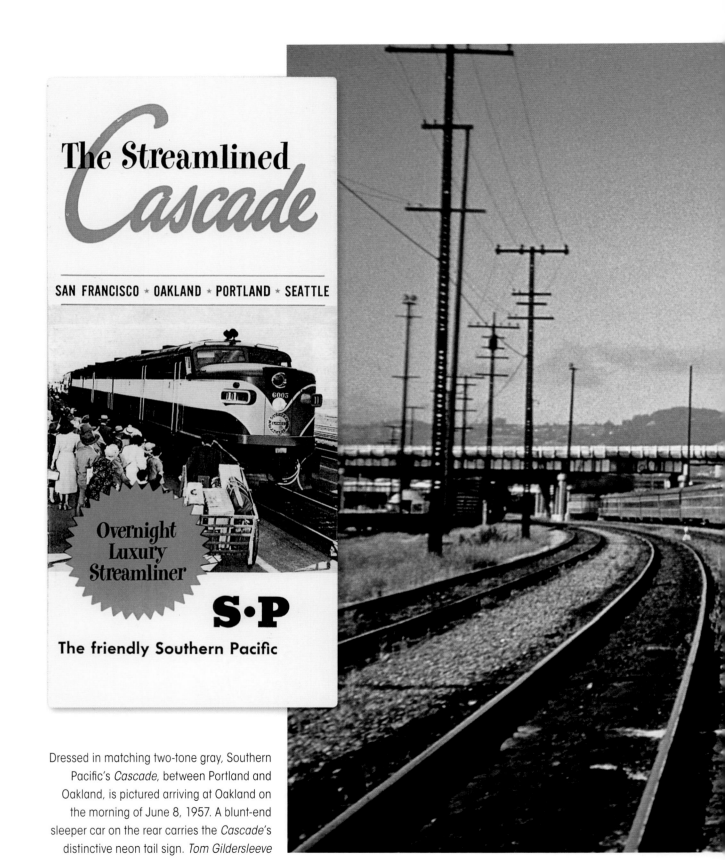

The Streamlined *Cascade*

SAN FRANCISCO ★ OAKLAND ★ PORTLAND ★ SEATTLE

6005

Overnight Luxury Streamliner

S·P

The friendly Southern Pacific

Dressed in matching two-tone gray, Southern Pacific's *Cascade*, between Portland and Oakland, is pictured arriving at Oakland on the morning of June 8, 1957. A blunt-end sleeper car on the rear carries the *Cascade*'s distinctive neon tail sign. *Tom Gildersleeve*

The Pullman Palette

AS FAR BACK AS THE MID-1800S, passenger cars were known for their spectacular and unique lettering and finishing as well as the craftsmanship of their interiors. Heavy coats of hand-rubbed paint and detailed gold-leaf ornamentation once graced the fleet of Pullman Palace cars as the company's fleet grew in the 1880s. However, undoubtedly in response to the gritty nature of railroading, the Pullman fleet of cars had long been painted a deep chocolate brown. That changed in 1900 when Pullman vice president, Thomas Wickes, asked the Pullman paint department to create a green color that would be suitable for a railroad environment. The result was Pullman green—identified as color number 70-10. Resistant to fading and carefully chosen to minimize the appearance of dirt, the dark green color became the standard for Pullman's massive fleet.

Thereafter, Pullman green number 70-10, adorned with rich gold-leaf lettering and set off by a black car roof and underbody could be found on the vast majority of Pullman cars operating for the first four decades of the twentieth century. As the Pullman fleet reached its zenith at over 9,000 cars in the mid-1930s, Pullman maintained only a handful of other special paint schemes: Tuscan red for cars assigned to the mighty Pennsylvania Railroad, orange and maroon for the Milwaukee Road, dark blue for four parlor cars assigned to the Wabash, red for two sleeping cars on the Tennessee Central, yellow and brown for a small group of the earliest streamlined sleeping cars assigned to Union Pacific, and stainless steel for a handful of Budd-built sleeping cars on the Santa Fe's famous *Super Chief* and Burlington's *Denver Zephyr*.

The rapid development and expansion of the streamlined train in the late 1930s brought with it a rainbow of color. Desperate to blunt the 40 percent drop in ridership resulting from the impacts of the auto and Great Depression, American railroads introduced sleek new trains finished in a range of vibrant hues. Baltimore & Ohio's blue and gray, Gulf, Mobile & Ohio's brilliant silver and red, Illinois Central's chocolate and orange, and a host of other paint schemes transformed the stodgy image of American railroading, seemingly overnight. By 1942, Pullman's "Descriptive List of Cars" noted the existence of 21 special paint schemes on their cars.

The colors often had significance to the territory of the local railroad. Indiana-based Monon painted its trains in the color scheme of the state's top universities. Likewise, Lehigh Valley, which served upstate New York, sported Cornell red. More often car paint schemes were created to match new diesel locomotives being delivered to haul passenger trains. Pullman passenger car paint schemes often complimented the work of the Electro-Motive Division of General Motors Styling Section or similar work done by Alco. High-powered industrial designers like Otto Kuhler, Raymond Loewy, and Henry Dreyfuss hired by large railroads shaped the color schemes of some of the country's most famous trains. Car builder Pullman-Standard expanded its color and design department in response to these trends.

World War II interrupted the development of new streamlined passenger trains, but the concept returned in earnest postwar. Building on the prewar movement, a large number of trains were streamlined after World War II. New paint schemes proliferated, sometimes with railroads operating cars with differing paint selections depending on the route to which they were assigned. Southern Pacific, for example, fielded two-tone gray cars on its *Lark* and *Cascade* trains linking cities along the Pacific Coast, yellow and red cars on its *City* fleet trains to Chicago (operated with Union Pacific and Chicago & North Western), red and silver on cars assigned to the *Golden State* train between Los Angeles, Arizona, and Chicago, and stainless steel with a red letter board on cars serving in the legendary *Sunset Limited* between Los Angeles and New Orleans. PRR, which participated in a number of through car operations by forwarding cars to

A Sampling of Major Railroad Pullman Paint Schemes, 1952

Atlantic Coast Line — Stainless steel, purple letterboard (lightweight cars), purple and silver with yellow lettering (heavyweight cars), or green (conventional cars)

Baltimore & Ohio — Blue and gray with yellow stripes or stainless steel with blue letterboard

Burlington — Stainless steel, black lettering (home road); see Great Northern and Northern Pacific for interline schemes

Chesapeake & Ohio — Gray and blue with yellow letterboard or stainless steel with yellow letter board and blue lettering

Chicago & North Western — Yellow and green with black stripes or two-tone gray with silver stripes (Overland Route service), or yellow and gray with red stripes (*City* fleet trains)

Erie — Green with gray pier panel

Florida East Coast — Stainless steel with black lettering

Frisco — Red simulated fluting (heavyweight cars) or red and stainless steel (lightweight cars)

Great Northern — Green and orange with gold stripes

Gulf, Mobile & Ohio — Maroon and red with gold stripes

Illinois Central — Orange and brown

Kansas City Southern — Dark green, yellow, and red

Katy — Red and simulated fluting (heavyweight cars) or red and stainless steel (lightweight cars)

Lackawanna — Gray and red with gold stripes or Pullman green (heavyweight cars)

Lehigh Valley — Cornell red

Louisville & Nashville — Blue or blue with simulated fluting (heavyweight cars), blue or blue with stainless steel (lightweight cars), stainless steel (for Southern Railway service), or Tuscan red (for Pennsylvania Railroad through service)

Milwaukee Road — Orange and red (maroon)

Missouri Pacific — Blue and gray with yellow stripes

New York Central — Two-tone gray with silver stripes, or stainless steel with black lettering

New Haven — Stainless steel with green window panels

Norfolk & Western — Tuscan red with gold stripes

Northern Pacific — Two-tone green with gold stripes

Pennsylvania Railroad — Tuscan red with gold stripes; blue and gray with yellow stripes (Missouri Pacific through service); red with simulated fluting (Frisco and Katy through service); two-tone gray with silver stripes (Overland Route service); stainless steel with purple letterboard (Atlantic Coast Line service); stainless steel (Southern Railway and Seaboard Air Line service); stainless steel with Tuscan red letterboard (*Congressional* and *Senator* trains); or yellow and gray with red stripes (Union Pacific/Southern Pacific *City* trains)

Rock Island — Red and silver (*Golden State*) or stainless steel with black lettering

Rio Grande — Orange and aluminum with black stripes or stainless steel (*California Zephyr*)

Santa Fe — Two-tone gray with silver stripes or stainless steel with black lettering

Seaboard Air Line — Pullman green or two-tone gray (heavyweight cars), maroon and gray (heavyweight *Orange Blossom Special*), or stainless steel (lightweight cars)

Southern Railway — Green (heavyweight cars) or stainless steel (lightweight cars)

Union Pacific — Two-tone gray with silver stripes (heavyweight and lightweight Overland Route service) or yellow and gray with red stripes (C&NW/Union Pacific/Southern Pacific *City* trains)

Wabash — Blue (heavyweight and lightweight cars), yellow and gray with red stripes (Union Pacific/Southern Pacific *City* trains), or blue with stainless steel (*City of Kansas City*)

Western Pacific — Stainless steel (lightweight cars)

Chicago and St. Louis for incorporation into the trains of other railroads going farther west, painted a number of its sleeping cars to match the colors of its partner railroads. Postwar, the PRR rostered lightweight Pullman cars in at least 11 different paint schemes!

Some measure of the proliferation in colors of postwar Pullman cars can be gleaned from a look at the 1952 Pullman list of "Exterior Painting Arrangements." Assembled to keep track of the subject during a time when Pullman's fleet contained thousands of both older heavyweight and newer lightweight cars, the list noted hundreds of distinct Pullman paint schemes in service on 46 different railroads, in addition to cars in Pullman's own pool.

Budd produced this brochure to promote its innovative Slumbercoach. *Budd Company photo*

continued from page 163

COMPETITION AND INNOVATION

Ironically, the introduction of all the new light-weight cars rendered Pullman's older heavyweight cars obsolete overnight in the minds of travelers. It was a big problem for Pullman, because heavyweight cars still made up the majority of its fleet into the early 1950s. For example, in 1951, two-thirds of Pullman's daily departures still occurred in heavyweight cars. As demand declined and heavyweight cars were rapidly retired, by 1956 only one-third of Pullman daily departures occurred in heavyweight cars. Like their predecessors, the new light-weight sleeping cars served every corner of the country.

Other changes were occurring simultaneously. Pullman found itself once more in a battle for revenue. As competition increased and America changed the way it traveled, the number of Pullman cars in service declined. In 1946, Pullman operated 5,500 cars, but by 1956 the fleet had been cut by more than half. Desperate to retain ridership in the face of cheaper airfares, the railroads and Pullman introduced the Slumbercoach in 1956. Actually, the concept of a budget sleeper had been at play for decades, as Pullman originally operated heavyweight tourist sleepers with 14 and 16 sections. The company also experimented with high-capacity cars. In 1925, Pullman tested a three-tiered budget sleeping car. In the early 1940s, Pullman introduced the coach-sleeping car, which slept up to 45 passengers. Postwar, the Budd Company had experimented with a 32-passenger Budgette car, American Car and Foundry had conceived the Slumberliner, while Pullman-Standard envisioned the 30-seat Railotel. None of these three early postwar budget concepts ever made it past the idea stage. Therefore, it was left to Budd to introduce a successful budget sleeper in 1956. The car offered 24 duplex rooms and 8 double rooms, and slept 40 passengers. Originally called the Siesta Coach by Budd and dubbed

Finished in a striking livery of dark green and orange, *Sheyenne River* contained no fewer than four different Pullman accommodations: 8 duplex roomettes, 4 sections, 3 bedrooms, and 1 compartment. The car was assigned to Great Northern's *Empire Builder* between Chicago and Seattle/Portland. *Harry Stegmaier collection*

the Slumbercoach by its first operator, CB&Q, the four CB&Q cars built in 1956 to Pullman Plan 9540 inspired the creation of two more Slumbercoaches in 1958 for use on the B&O *Columbian* and 12 additional cars in 1959. Four cars were leased to MP and B&O for assignment to the *National Limited* and *Texas Eagle* between Washington and San Antonio. One car went to MP and three went to B&O. NYC received four cars that were originally assigned to the *20th Century Limited* and the *New England States*, while Northern Pacific's original four Slumbercoaches served on the road's *North Coast Limited* between Chicago and Seattle. Pullman operated and staffed all but the NYC cars. Indeed, NYC was so impressed with the concept that it sent 10 of its 22-roomette sleeping cars back to Budd in 1961 to be rebuilt into similar 16-roomette, 10-economy-room sleepers. In 1964, the lease expired on the MP, B&O, and NYC 24-8 cars. They along with the four original NP-leased cars were sold to NP. They were used on the railroad's *North Coast Limited* and *Mainstreeter*.

Despite their innovative design, the Slumbercoaches proved to be the last new Pullman-operated sleeping car design created in company history. By the late 1960s, the speed of the airplane and convenience of the automobile had defeated the private railroad passenger train. Nevertheless, the postwar lightweight era was one of the most innovative and interesting periods in Pullman's history. Facing overwhelming competition, the company responded by introducing the most beautiful passenger equipment in history. Coupled with the fact that the company never compromised its high level of onboard service, it was the best time in history to "Go Pullman."

On May 1, 1971, most American railroads ceased operating their own intercity passenger trains. Amtrak, a new national carrier funded by the government, continued passenger service in the United States with a skeletal network and reduced roster of cars. Within that roster were hundreds of cars once operated by the world's greatest first-class transportation provider—The Pullman Company.

ACKNOWLEDGMENTS

The century-long history of the Pullman car fleet is complex. A number of people generously shared their time, knowledge, and collections to make this a better book. The following individuals deserve special mention for assistance above and beyond the call of duty.

Harry Stegmaier opened his renowned photo collection to the authors, hand-selecting images for the book. We are much indebted to Chuck Blardone, who offered critical technical assistance despite a hectic schedule. Steve Esposito and the staff of Andover Junction Publications pitched in to help recover rare images from Pullman's archival company films. Art Peterson provided outstanding and rare color images of Pullman cars. Rob McGonigal, editor of Kalmbach Publishing's *Classic Trains*, opened Kalmbach's David P. Morgan Library to the authors. Greg Ames, curator of the John W. Barriger III National Railroad Library at the University of Missouri–St. Louis, came up with choice images of Pullman's passenger car fleet. Bob Schmidt provided numerous wonderful images from his own collection. Bill Stauss, an expert on Pullman cars, sent photos from his collection as well as photos of his outstanding car models. Ralph Barger and Bob Wayner, experts on Pullman, took their time to educate the authors in person and through their own publications. Larry Thomas came through with last-minute material. Tom Madden's exhaustive Pullman research project proved invaluable. Stacey Borland provided timely and expert proofreading of the body of the text. Dennis Pernu of Voyageur Press navigated us through the contract and the writing process.

As you leaf through the pages of this book you will find an array of photos, advertising, information, and art that tells the story of a great American company and its equipment. The following individuals and organizations are due a big thank-you for taking the images, providing the material, or assisting the authors in acquiring it: ACF Industries, Chuck Blardone, Bob's Photos, John Bromley, Gehritt Bruins, California State Railroad Museum, Donald Duke, Tom Gildersleeve, S. C. Gregory, J. Michael Gruber, M. Herson, Dave Ingles, Kalmbach Publishing, Bob Liljestrand, Bill Olson, The Pennsylvania Railroad Technical and Historical Society, Art Peterson, Dean Ralston, Railway & Locomotive Historical Society, Bob Schmidt, Jim Scribbins, Larry Thomas, Union Pacific Railroad, and Union Pacific Railroad Museum.

Also due a debt of gratitude are the many photographers (and companies) now gone who created such a wonderful visual history, including Alan Bradley, the Budd Company, Chicago & North Western Railroad, W. B. Cox, Alfred W. Johnson, George Krambles, Russell Luedke, R. V. Mehlenbeck, Dan Peterson, Russ Porter, Bill Price, the Pullman Company, Pullman-Standard Car Manufacturing Company, A. M. Rung, Santa Fe Railway, and Southern Pacific Railroad.

Last but not least, our families deserve our thanks. Very special thanks to Janis, Jennifer, Kevin, Katie, Kellie, Graeme, and Russell for their patience and support!

BIBLIOGRAPHY

BOOKS

Barger, Ralph. *A Century of Pullman Cars, Volume 1*. Sykesville, Md.: Greenberg Publishing Co., 1988.

———. *A Century of Pullman Cars, Volume 2*. Sykesville, Md.: Greenberg Publishing Co., 1990.

Beebe, Lucius, and Charles Clegg. *The Trains We Rode, Volume 1*. Berkeley, Calif.: Howell-North Books, 1965

———. *The Trains We Rode, Volume 2*. Berkeley, Calif.: Howell-North Books, 1966.

Blardone, Charles Jr., and Peter Tilp. *Pennsylvania Railroad Passenger Car Painting and Lettering*. Upper Darby, Pa.: Pennsylvania Railroad Technical & Historical Society, 1988.

Dubin, Arthur. *More Classic Trains*. Milwaukee, Wis.: Kalmbach Publishing, 1974.

———. *Some Classic Trains*. Milwaukee, Wis.: Kalmbach Publishing, 1964.

Frailey, Fred. *Twilight of the Great Trains*. Milwaukee, Wis.: Kalmbach Publishing, 1998.

Husband, Joseph. *The Story of the Pullman Car*. Chicago: A. C. McClurg Co., 1917.

Luckin, Richard. *Dining on Rails*. Golden, Colo.: RK Publications, 1983.

Randall, David. *Streamliner Cars, Volume 1*. Godfrey, Ill.: RPC Publications, 1981.

———. *Streamliner Cars, Volume 2*. Godfrey, Ill.: RPC Publications, 1981.

———. *Streamliner Cars, Volume 3*. Godfrey, Ill.: RPC Publications, 1982.

Southern Pacific Passenger Cars, Volume 2. Pasadena, Calif.: Southern Pacific Historical & Technical Society, 2005.

Wayner, Robert. *Car Names Numbers and Consists*. New York, N.Y.: Wayner Publications, 1972.

———. *The Complete Roster of Heavyweight Pullman Cars*. New York, N.Y.: Wayner Publications, 1985.

Welsh, Joe, and Bill Howes. *Travel by Pullman*. St. Paul, Minn.: MBI Publishing Co., 2004

Welsh, Joseph M. *By Streamliner: New York to Florida*. Andover, N.J.: Andover Junction Publications, 1994.

White, John H. Jr., *The American Railroad Passenger Car*. Baltimore, Md.: The Johns Hopkins University Press, 1978.

OTHER SOURCES

Railway Age magazine.

Tower, Richard L. Jr., "A Hog Can Cross America Without Changing Trains—But You Can't!" A presentation to the Lexington Group in Transportation History, September 27, 1996.

Pullman descriptive lists of cars (various years).

INDEX